WHATEVER BECAME OF . . . ?

Fourth Series

Also by the Author

WHATEVER BECAME OF . . . ?

Fourth Series

by
RICHARD LAMPARSKI

CROWN PUBLISHERS, INC., NEW YORK

Acknowledgments

The author would like to express thanks to the following people who helped in the preparation of this book: Michael Knowles (a colleague), Dick Lynch, Don Miller, Cinemabilia, Kirk Crivello, Marvin Paige, Charles Higham, Jon Virzi, Joe Riccuiti, Don Koll, Danny Frank, *Movie Star News,* George Eells, De Witt Bodeen, Curtis Harrington, Tony Slyde, Wayne Clark, Robert G. Youngson, Jeanne Youngson, Leonard Maltin, *Film Fan Monthly,* John Robbins, Ene Riisna, Anselma Dell 'Olio, Joseph O'Donohue IV, Ellis St. Joseph, Malcolm Leo, Chris Albertson, Helen Bernstein, and Burt Braff.

Individuals whose names are footnoted (1, 2, or 3) in the text appear as separate segments in previous volumes in this series. Footnote 1 refers to Volume One of *Whatever Became of . . . ?*, footnote 2 refers to *Whatever Became of . . . ? Second Series,* and footnote 3 refers to *Whatever Became of . . . ? Third Series.*

Printed in the United States of America
Published simultaneously in Canada by General Publishing Company Limited
Third Printing, April, 1974

For Diane Arbus (1923–1971)
who did so much to raise the standards
of her art and the consciousness of us all

CONTENTS

In Alphabetical Order

Left to right: Moe, Curly, and Larry defied by a dog.

THE THREE STOOGES

The surviving members of the comic trio are Moe Harry Howard, born in 1905 in Brooklyn, and Larry Fine, born on October 5, 1902, in Philadelphia.

Moe, who had been a bit player in early silent films, had performed on a riverboat, and acted in Shakespeare, then joined the famous vaudeville headliner Ted Healy in 1922. Moe's brother Sam, known as Shemp, heckled Moe and Healy from the audience—until Healy hired him about a year later when Shemp walked on stage during a performance, mashed a pear in Healy's face, and brought the house down. Moe's older partner, Larry, who was part of a flash act in vaudeville, made it a threesome in 1925. They were billed variously as Ted Healy and His Gang, Ted Healy and His Racketeers, and Ted Healy and His Three Southern Gentlemen before settling on Ted Healy and His Three Stooges. Healy went on as a single when the Stooges began making pictures.

They made their movie debut in a 1930 Rube Goldberg feature, *Soup to Nuts,* and then went to M-G-M where they made a brief appearance in several features, including *Dancing Lady* (1933) , and a few shorts. By this time, Shemp had decided to work as a single and was replaced by the youngest of the Howard boys, Jerry, who the family called Babe. He's the one movie fans know as Curly and he was without doubt the star of the act until illness caused his departure in 1946. Shemp returned to replace Curly, who died in 1952.

The Stooges were brought to Columbia Pictures by Jules White, who directed many of their two-reelers, beginning with *Woman Haters* (1934) . Two others who guided their nonsense were Del Lord and the comic star of silents, Charlie Chase.

8

They looked ridiculous. Grown men, one fat, dumb, and completely bald; Moe bossing everyone around while wearing a Buster Brown haircut; and Larry, a ball of hair behind each ear adding to his look of annoyance and confusion. Kids loved the Stooges, and on matinee day in low-income neighborhoods in the thirties and forties their shorts were advertised on the marquees right along with the features.

The Stooges remained on the Gower Street lot through 190 starring shorts, finishing their last on January 12, 1958, but without Shemp. He had died suddenly in 1955, and was replaced first by Joe Besser for three years and, when he left, Joe De Rita took over. But the chemistry worked with neither one, and although the Stooges continued to make personal appearances and an occasional feature, including *Snow White and the Three Stooges* (1961) and *The Three Stooges Meet Hercules* (1963), the humor seemed forced.

The Stooges' shorts, however, were always consistent money-makers for their studio, whose chief Harry Cohn was one of their biggest fans. Although the sound effects and customary incongruous situations were missing at their in-person dates at presentation houses during their heyday, Stooges fans were convulsed anyway when the three sang songs like "She Was Bred in Old Kentucky, but She's Just a Crumb Up Here."

Larry is a widower and lives at the Motion Picture Country House. Moe and his wife, whose cousin was the legendary Houdini, live in a modern house above the Sunset Strip in West Hollywood. Larry and Moe are delighted that their pictures have proved so popular on TV as well as having played in almost every country in the world. However, the Soviets, who requested the films, were turned down when it was learned that they intended to use them to depict Americans being brutalized by eye gouging, kicks in the shin, and twisted noses in the name of fun.

Moe in his home above the Sunset Strip. *Mary Kay Carlson*

Larry at the Motion Picture Country House in Woodland Hills, California. *Jeanne Youngson*

Rosa giving Shirley Temple a singing lesson in 1935.

ROSA PONSELLE

"The greatest single voice in any category" is how the music critic of the *New York Times* recently described Rosa. She was born Rosa Ponzillo on January 22, 1897, in Meriden, Connecticut. Rosa's Italian immigrant father was a coal and ice dealer.

Rosa and her sister Carmela, who is five years older, began their careers singing in a New Haven tavern frequented by Yale students. By the time Rosa was twenty-one, the Ponselles' sister act was on the vaudeville bill at the Palace Theatre in New York City. William Thorner, a voice coach, was told of the pair and went to see if the extravagant praise he had heard was remotely true. Rosa's sound and beauty dazzled him and he felt she might be the Leonora sought by the Metropolitan Opera to sing opposite Enrico Caruso in the revival of *La Forza del Destino*. Both Caruso and the Met management were impressed. What everyone found even more extraordinary, though, was that Rosa had not had any vocal training, and she refused it thereafter.

She made her debut on November 15, 1918, as Leonora and set new standards at the Met, which many opera fans think have never been equaled. Her favorite role was Carmen but she was equally brilliant in *Norma, La Traviata, Cavalleria Rusticana,* and *La Gioconda.* Her repertory of twenty-two roles was as astonishing as her voice. To the delight of buffs, she sang operas that were then obscure, and almost forgotten today; *L'Africaine, Fedra,* and *The Legend* starring Ponselle packed the house as easily as such of her well-known vehicles as *Andrea Chénier* and *Don Carlos.*

However, before the 1937–38 season she asked to do *Adriana Lecouvreur.* She was refused, and left the Metropolitan, never again to set foot inside, even to see a performance. In 1937, Rosa and her husband, Carle A. Jackson, moved to Baltimore where his father had been mayor. Their fourteen-year marriage ended in a 1950 divorce. The diva not only left the Met but her recording and radio career as well. There was some talk of her making films but nothing came of it.

Considering that in the minds of most she was the greatest prima donna of her time, the stories of her temperament are few. Rosa insisted that the stage be unheated and the management complied, although other artists complained that a cold stage was a danger to their throats as well as uncomfortable. However, she mastered difficult roles quickly, her acting was more than satisfactory, she could take the low notes of a contralto, and her high C was sublime. Added to all that was one of the last qualities then required of a great soprano: she was very sexy. In the words of musicologist Harold C. Schonberg, "She seemed to have everything." And yet Rosa never gave a performance that she was not tortured with nervousness for hours before.

When the Metropolitan gave Giovanni Martinelli[2] a gala a few years before his death, the tenor implored his old friend Rosa to join him in the celebration. Those pleas as well as the ones from director Rudolf Bing to attend the closing of the old house and the opening of the new one were to no avail. As far as anyone knows, Rosa Ponselle has not been to New York since she left over three decades ago.

She is, however, by no means a recluse. She is very active in the affairs of the Baltimore Opera, of which she is a director. She is surrounded at all times by her many toy poodles and much of the time by an endless parade of single, young men who are devoted to her, although they only know the legendary voice from her old records. She is paid occasional visits by Carmela, who lives in Manhattan. Her sister sang now and then with Rosa at the Met but, like almost everyone else who appeared with Rosa, was forever in her shadow.

Madame Ponselle on her last birthday at Villa Pace. *The New York Times*

In uniform for his 1944 appearance
in *Winged Victory*.

LON McCALLISTER

The clean-cut young American boy actor was born Herbert Alonzo McCallister, Jr., in Los Angeles on April 17, 1923. In 1928 his parents were divorced and a year later his grandparents, who had done very well in real estate, were wiped out by the stock market crash. At a very early age he set two goals: to make a lot of money in the movies and to quit by the time he was thirty. He retired at twenty-nine with two apartment houses and a Malibu Beach house that was fit for any movie star.

Lon had taken singing, riding, and acting lessons, and studied tap dancing at the Fanchon & Marco School (Fanchon is dead; Marco Wolf is a practitioner of Christian Science in Los Angeles).

It was *Romeo and Juliet* that brought him luck—twice. He auditioned for and got his first part in a movie, the 1936 *Romeo and Juliet,* singing with the Maxwell Choristers. The film starred Norma Shearer[1] and Leslie Howard. Then, under the name Buddy McCallister, which he later changed to Bud, he worked as an extra, a dress extra, a bit player, and a stand-in in about a hundred pictures, including *Stella Dallas* (1937), *Babes in Arms* (1939), and *Always in My Heart* (1942). He was one of hundreds of actors to read for the role of the soldier who plays a scene from *Romeo and Juliet* opposite Katharine Cornell[2] in her only screen appearance. The movie was *Stage Door Canteen* (1943). It was crammed with stars and was a box office smash of the war years. Lon learned of his landing the part by reading Hedda Hopper's column which announced that the grandson of the RKO studio gateman was chosen. The producer, Sol Lesser, at that point changed McCallister's name to Lon and placed him under contract.

Lon got a deferral on his induction into the Signal Corps to make the charming *Home in Indiana* (1944), and a long leave for his part in *Winged Victory* (1944), with Edmond O'Brien (married to Olga San Juan). He was one of the favorite young actors among fan magazine readers, and his appearances in such pictures as *The Red House* (1947), *Scudda Hoo!*

Scudda Hay! (1948), and *The Story of Seabiscuit* (1949) were always well publicized. He referred recently to his last few films, *A Yank in Korea* (1951), *Montana Territory* (1952), and *Combat Squad* (1953), as "not enjoyable to make," but he was well paid for them.

When he left motion pictures Lon got on a freighter with his close friend the late actor William Eythe and went to South America where they made several travel films. These eventually were sold to airlines and for stock footage. Lon did a lot of traveling and settled for a few years in London before returning to Los Angeles in 1960.

The star who was once hailed as "the young Richard Barthelmess" is still a bachelor. He takes frequent trips on his sailboat and in his motor home. His Malibu house he rents to such luminaries as Roger Vadim and Jason Robards, Jr., while he lives in one of the units of his Hollywood apartment house.

Although he laughs heartily whenever someone suggests he act again, McCallister is very loyal to the Hollywood that made him a star, and intends to leave everything he owns to the Motion Picture Country House. Throughout the years he has kept in close touch with Deanna Durbin, David Manners,[1] Madge Kennedy (living in Los Angeles), and Buddy Pepper. Two of his closest friends are Jane Withers (who continues to do the cleanser TV commercial) and George Cukor.

Although he starred in only eleven feature films, Lon is among the top ten actors inquired about by fans of the Hollywood of yesterday. When told of his popularity he replied that he was "stunned and very grateful." Says Lon: "I hope they know that when I worked in pictures I did the best I could. It wasn't very good at times but I really tried." His life today he describes as being a happy, anonymous existence. "Every single day I have a hell of a good time with all the simple pleasures a movie star never can indulge in. When I think of all the things I'm grateful for, the safety of my privacy heads the list."

Friends call him Bud these days.
Ray Foster

In her heyday, considered the most beautiful woman in pictures.

HEDY LAMARR

The star once considered the most beautiful woman in motion pictures was born Hedwig Eva Maria Kiesler in Vienna, Austria, on November 9, 1913. Her parents were well off and they adored their only child. But until she was in her early teens, Hedy was thought of as an ugly duckling. Her nose was much too small. Although her parents didn't approve, she was permitted to appear in a few plays and films, such as *Man Braucht Kein Geld* (1932). They were appalled, however, when *Ecstasy* (1937) was released and moviegoers all over the world saw their daughter romping through the woods stark naked and being made love to. Her first husband, munitions king Fritz Mandl, tried desperately to buy up all the prints. Although he spent a fortune trying, the film still exists. The Mandls' nightmarish marriage ended in a 1937 divorce after Hedy escaped his house disguised as a maid. She fled to Paris.

Shortly after, Louis B. Mayer signed her to an M-G-M contract at $500 a week, and he changed her name. Audiences and critics found her dazzling in her Hollywood debut, *Algiers* (1938). But aside from allowing the public to look at her in features like *Boom Town* (1940), *Tortilla Flat* (1942), *White Cargo* (1942), and *Experiment Perilous* (1944), Hollywood didn't seem to know what to do with the Continental beauty.

Her own judgment seemed even worse. She turned down the leads in *Laura, Saratoga Trunk,* and *Gaslight,* and after she formed her own production company she made two mediocre features, *The Strange Woman* (1946) and *Dishonored Lady* (1947). Everyone else had given up on Hedy when Cecil B. de Mille cast her in the title role of *Samson and Delilah* (1949). It was followed by others—*Copper Canyon* (1950), *My Favorite Spy* (1951), and the Italian flop, *The Face That Launched a Thousand*

Ships (1953), and then nothing—until she appeared as Joan of Arc in the failure *The Story of Mankind* (1957). There were several announcements about upcoming movies, which were never made, and one that was made but never released.

She has stopped acting in films, but her fans have been able to keep up with her activities. She was married to rich man Ted Stauffer from 1951 until 1952 and to rich man Lee Howard (now married to Gene Tierney and living in Houston) from 1953 to 1959. Then there was a two-year marriage to an attorney. Preceding these three of course were Mandl; her second husband, screenwriter Gene Markey (married to the owner of Calumet Farms and living in Lexington, Kentucky); and her third, John Loder. Just before Hedy's autobiography, *Ecstasy and Me,* was published in 1966, she was denied a court injunction to stop it. Since then, she has denied much of its contents and has been suing everyone concerned for $21 million. The year before, she had made front pages when she was arrested after leaving the May Company department store in Los Angeles. She had some articles she had neglected to pay for. Although a jury dismissed the charges, she lost the lead in a B film, *Picture Mommy Dead,* to Zsa Zsa Gabor a few days later. In 1969, her adopted son, James, a policeman in Omaha, shot and killed a fourteen-year-old black girl.

For the last few years, she has been living in New York City. Hedy is so involved in legal actions that litigation has become a way of life for her. As for the money she made, by her own count, she has gone through about $30 million.

Her behavior, which is guided greatly by her horoscope, has long baffled close friends, who claim she is more intelligent and amusing than her performances ever indicated. The key might be found in a line of her book: "After a taste of stardom, everything else is poverty."

At a recent party held in a Broadway delicatessen. *New York Daily News*

With Gloria Swanson, dressed for the Barn Dance Party given at Hollywood's Café Vendome by Kay Francis, 1933.

ZEPPO MARX

Zeppo, Marx Brother No. 4, was born to Sam and Minnie Marx (an unsuccessful tailor and the very ambitious daughter of a German magician) in the Yorkville section of Manhattan on February 25, 1901.

Zeppo joined his brothers sixteen years later just when their act was beginning to catch on in vaudeville circuits around the country. He always felt inadequate, and whether he played Groucho's son, or the romantic lead or the nominal hero, he always looked like what he was—a relative. Zeppo probably escaped being dubbed a fifth wheel only because there already was a fifth son, Gummo, who, Marx Brother fans remember, left the act long before they made it big in movies.

In the Brothers' first big Broadway hit, *I'll Say She Is* (1924), Zeppo was still being billed as Herbert, his real name. He was in their other two stage successes, *The Cocoanuts* (1925) and *Animal Crackers* (1928), under the name Zeppo. When the boys played London's Palace in *Varieties* in 1931, Zeppo was along.

The Marx Brothers debuted on the screen for Paramount in *The Cocoanuts* (1929) and created a sensation. They stuck together for four more pictures: *Animal Crackers* (1930), *Monkey Business* (1931), *Horse Feathers* (1932), and *Duck Soup* (1933). Although these are rated by most fans as some of their best work, Zeppo seems quite nonessential in all. He wasn't good-looking enough to be believable as the lover and he remained unfunny throughout.

When his brothers moved to M-G-M in 1934 Zeppo made his decision to leave. At first he joined the agentry office of Orsatti & Brene in Hollywood.

Later he opened his own very successful stable of stars in New York City. For a time Gummo was one of his partners. A few of the clients he represented until he retired twenty years ago were Lucille Ball, Barbara Stanwyck, George S. Kaufman, and Fred MacMurray. Asked once why he didn't handle his brothers, Zeppo replied that he had set the deal for them to appear in *Room Service* (1928), for which they were paid $250,000. Groucho informed him that they should have gotten $350,000, and with that he dropped the account.

He has never for a minute regretted his split with the team, and his life since then has certainly never lacked for excitement. In 1952 he engaged in a fistfight with producer Alex Gottlieb, during which Mrs. Gottlieb, the sister of Billy Rose, was knocked to the ground. In 1954 Zeppo and his wife of twenty-seven years were divorced. She is the former Marian Benda, who had been in the cast of their show *The Cocoanuts* on Broadway. In 1955 Zeppo was sued for $300,000 when his son Tim hit a neighbor's child with a rock. In 1958 Zeppo was questioned by a federal grand jury regarding a large betting ring; also that year he got into a brawl at the Mocambo, and later announced his engagement to nineteen-year-old model-singer Diane Davis. Instead of marrying Miss Davis, the following year he wed model Barbara Blakely. In 1968 he sued Debbie Reynolds's husband, Harry Karl, for $449,000 over some stock in nicotineless cigarettes. Zeppo is a heavy smoker. In 1972, he and Barbara separated and she began dating Frank Sinatra.

The second youngest Marx brother lives in Palm Springs practically next door to Gummo, the baby of the family, and near Groucho. Chico and Harpo, like their famous foil, Margaret Dumont, are dead. Zeppo has a large boat in San Diego, which he uses for sailing and fishing. His other occupation is golf. But pet aversions are interviews and being photographed, which are offset by a new interest—inventing; he holds patent no. 3,426,747 on a wristwatch that along with telling the time checks on the wearer's heartbeat.

A reluctant Zeppo sits for his photograph in Hollywood. *John P. Gilligan*

Billed for a time as the "Most Beautiful Woman in the World."

VERA HRUBA RALSTON

The former "Queen of Republic Pictures" was born Vera Hruba in Prague on June 12, 1921. When she was twelve her brother Rudy convinced her to concentrate her considerable energies on ice skating rather than on classical ballet, which she had been studying since she was four. One year later Vera was champion of Prague.

In the Berlin Olympics of 1936 she finished second to Sonja Henie[1] but made international headlines when Hitler asked her how she would like to skate for the Swastika. "I'd rather skate on it!" she replied to a livid Fuerher.

Vera was on the last plane to fly out of Prague when the Nazis marched into the Sudetenland. She arrived in New York with $30 and landed a job with an ice revue at the Hotel New Yorker. Then came a two-year tour with Ice Vanities before being signed as a principal with Ice Capades.

Vera was taking acting lessons from Josephine Dillon (Clark Gable's first wife) when she was signed to a long-term contract with Republic Pictures. This was after appearances in *Ice Capades* (1941) and *Ice Capades Revue* (1942).

Billed as Vera Hruba Ralston, who "skated out of Czechoslovakia into the hearts of America," she appeared in *The Lady and the Monster* (1944) and *Lake Placid Serenade* (1944). The latter had a plot not unlike her own story. Her billing in *The Lady and the Plainsman* (1946) was minus the Hruba (the "H" is silent). Among her other films are *Wyoming* (1947), with the late Gabby (George) Hayes, *Angel on the Amazon* (1948), in which she played a woman who had been frightened by a panther and could never age, *I, Jane Doe* (1948) her personal favorite, *Fair Wind to Java* (1953), *Spoilers of the Forest* (1957), with Hillary Brooke (Mrs. Ray Klune of San Luis Rey Downs, California), and her swan song, *The Man Who Died Twice* (1958).

All of Vera's features were made at Republic, a lot never known for an A product. The studio's president, Herbert J. Yates, however, took a personal interest in her career from the beginning, and veteran employees were amazed at just how much he was willing to spend on his star. Republic stockholders were somewhat differently impressed, and in 1956 their objections took the form of a lawsuit that claimed that Sterling Hayden was hired "at an improvident and excessive salary to induce him to appear with Miss Ralston" in *Timberjack* (1955). It was alleged that John Wayne refused to work with her after their two costarring vehicles bombed at the box office. In fact, said the suit, only two of Vera's twenty features had even made back their negative costs.

Yates and Vera, who was forty years his junior, were married in March, 1952. Until he was deposed at Republic in a 1958 proxy fight, he continued to indulge her in production values usually found only in lavish movies made on major lots. He saw to it until he died in 1966 that she had a lifestyle on par with any of Hollywood's reigning queens. Her large collection of his expensive gifts includes a diamond bracelet she discovered one night inside her broiled trout.

The former star lives alone in Santa Barbara's exclusive Hope Ranch in a mansion complete with full-time help, watchdogs, and a $5,000 whirlpool bath. She inherited half of Yates's estate, which was valued at over $10 million.

Always personally popular on her home lot, Vera sees many of those who worked on her twenty-eight films, including costar John Carroll. She has begun to travel some after several years' illness during which she could not even walk. She attributes her recovery to faith healer Oral Roberts.

The woman whose name exhibitors once refused to place on their marquees is ready for her comeback. She allowed in a recent interview that she did not believe she was ever used properly in pictures and is considering offers. Her heavy accent, which was one of the reasons that caused her to be dubbed the Queen of the Clinkers, is considerably lighter. And that makes her believe that the time is right for her to pursue her real forte—light comedy.

At a recent party she gave. *Rudy Ralston*

"SLAPSIE" MAXIE ROSENBLOOM

The Runyonesque character who reigned for several decades as a champion prizefighter and then movie comedian was born in New York City in 1903. His mother, who had been a dancer, sent him to ballet class and when the boys at the local pool hall began tipping their hats at him his boxing skill emerged by instinct. According to Maxie, he was sentenced to eighteen months at the Hawthorne Reform Home for Jewish Boys after he hit a public school teacher in the face when she attempted to spank his bare behind with a ruler. "My first knockout," said Maxie years later.

Upon Maxie's release from Hawthorne, George Raft[3] became interested in him and began grooming him for the ring. In 1921, while still an amateur, Maxie won the New York State middleweight, lightheavyweight, and heavyweight titles. Out of 410 fights during his career, Maxie had close to 400 victories. During the four years he held the World Light Heavyweight Championship, 1930–34, he fought a record 106 bouts. His habit of training on "apple pie and late hours" lost him the title to Bob Olin in Madison Square Garden in 1934. Early in Maxie's professional career. because of his cuffing, backhanded style Damon Runyon, then a sports writer, named him "Slapsie" Maxie.

Slapsie Maxie made his screen debut in *Mr. Broadway* (1933). In a test he had made for Warner Brothers he folded back one of his cauliflower ears while talking on the phone to a pal. The studio signed him and sent him to Max Reinhardt's school to study diction, but somehow it never showed in the dozens of films he made. Maxie always played a punch-drunk fighter, a hoodlum, or a good-natured dumbbell in features such as *Nothing Sacred* (1937), *My Son, the Hero* (1943), *Harvard, Here I Come* (1942), with Arline Judge (single and living in Hollywood), *Louisiana Purchase*

(1941), with Vera Zorina,[3] *Irish Eyes Are Smiling* (1945), with Dick Haymes,[2] *Mr. Universe* (1951), with the late Jack Carson, *Abbott & Costello Meet the Keystone Kops* (1955), and *The Beat Generation* (1959).

His tough-guy manner and "dees-and-dems" speech served him well during the 1950s in several road company versions of *Guys and Dolls* and on such TV shows as "The Damon Runyon Theatre" and "Eloise."

Slapsie Maxie hasn't done so well since. He admits to having gone through several million dollars, mostly on gambling; horse races were his particular specialty. In 1957 he was in a scrape with a thirteen-year-old girl. (A well publicized and messy divorce in 1945 had ended his six-year marriage to child psychologist Muriel Falder.) His quick wit, which was always well peppered with contrived malaprops, completely left him—just as did the freeloaders who used to hang around.

In 1970, he actually met with the California Boxing Commission to see about a comeback. The embarrassed official explained to the former champ that there was nothing in the laws to prevent a man of sixty-five from fighting if he could get a match.

With the lush nine years of his nightclub on L.A.'s Wilshire Boulevard and the weekly $1,000 salary in the forties from Columbia Pictures a distant memory for the last twenty years he could be found in the bar or the lobby of a hotel near Hollywood Boulevard and Vine Street. Of the single room he occupied at the hotel, he explained to an interviewer: "I only pay $100 a month, less than anyone else here. The hotel wants to keep me livin' here, see, cause I bring in the tourists. People from out of town, they like to see movie stars." Shortly after, the hotel was sold, for razing. Maxie has moved to a senior citizen home in Pasadena.

The ex-champ at home, Christmastime. *Donna Schaeffer*

A typical pose and expression, 1943.

CASS DALEY

The comedienne who made a career out of buck teeth and a large rear end was born Katherine Daley on July 17, 1915, in North Philadelphia, Pennsylvania. Her father was a streetcar conductor for over forty years. In her early teens she had to drop out of school for all but one day a week so she could help her family by working as a candy wrapper, a stocking trimmer, and in a hosiery mill. Her top wages during this period was $12 a week.

One Saturday night, in 1933, friends insisted that Cass perform during an amateur show in Gloucester City, New Jersey. She had quite a reputation for making people laugh and had once lost a job for mimicking the foreman. But in her debut she sang "Please Don't Talk About Me When I'm Gone," accompanying herself on the ukelele, and until that moment had never thought of going into show business. She has never considered anything else since.

For the next few years Cass went from nightclub hatcheck girl/singer to singer at a Walk-a-thon (which was emceed by an unknown Red Skelton). Next came the vaudeville circuits and presentation houses, where she sang briefly with Ozzie Nelson's band. She replaced Judy Canova[1] in the *Ziegfeld Follies of 1936,* which also featured June Preisser (living in Florida), and then toured the music halls of Great Britain. In 1939 she was back on Broadway with Joe Penner in *Yokel Boy.*

By this time Cass had learned to capitalize on a face and figure that would have ruined the life of another woman. In school, she had been told her teeth were so big she could eat corn on the cob through a tennis racket, and so in her early act she had tried to sing blues without showing her teeth. Now she featured her teeth every time she opened her mouth, and made sure no one missed her generous backside. The audiences were convulsed.

Cass signed with Paramount Pictures in 1941, just about the time she began to click on radio on such shows as "Maxwell House Coffee Time." She pinch-hit several times for comedienne Joan Davis and even replaced radio's "Fitch Bandwagon" one summer with her own show. It was on radio that she popularized the expression, "I said it and I'm glad!" Unfortunately, the studio took 50 percent of all her radio and personal appearance earnings.

Her screen debut, *The Fleet's In* (1942), was probably her best film, although her favorite is *Riding High* (1943), with Glenn Langan (living in Encino, California, with his wife Adele Jergens). Among her eleven others were *Crazy House* (1943), with Martha O'Driscoll (now Mrs. Arthur Appleton of Chicago), *Variety Girl* (1947), with Olga San Juan (living in Brentwood, California, with husband Edmond O'Brien), *Here Comes the Groom* (1951), and then, after a thirteen-year hiatus, *The Spirit Is Willing* (1967), followed by *Norwood* (1971), with Jack Haley.[3]

By the time her seven-year Paramount contract had expired, Cass had borne a son by her husband-manager Frank Kinsella. "We were living in Newport Beach, which is quite a drive from Hollywood," she said recently, "and you know what it's like out here—out of sight, out of mind!" She admits too that she never really tried very hard to find work on television, which would have been the perfect medium for her visual, broad comedy.

Cass and her husband have a small apartment a few blocks from her old studio. She continued her non-show-biz life as wife and mother until a couple of years ago when, "frankly, I ran out of money." In 1971 she did *The Music Man* in St. Louis and toured with *The Big Show of 1936* in 1972. She was seen not long ago on TV on a Nu-Soft (an ironing product) commercial. But "the casting people today don't know me or my work and when I tell them, they don't seem to care," says Cass today. The interpreter of a raucous, man-starved female who by her own description is "really dullsville," has surprised herself by collecting unemployment insurance for several quarters. As for the baby that interrupted her career, he was a volunteer for Richard Nixon in 1972 after his parents put him through law school and had his buck teeth straightened.

With Michael Knowles (author Lamparski's associate). *Diana Keyt*

About 1934.

GEORGE O'BRIEN

The "he-man" star of the twenties and thirties was born on April 19, 1900, in San Francisco where his father was chief of police and later police commissioner. George excelled at basketball, swimming, riding, and football. He missed out on boxing when his mother's pleadings kept him from accepting an offer from Jack Dempsey's manager to guide his career as a professional boxer.

After he left the Navy in 1919, cowboy star Tom Mix hired him at $15 a week to act as second assistant cameraman. Until then he had all but made up his mind to be a doctor. George left Mix after a year and bummed around Hollywood working as a lifeguard, extra, bit player, stuntman, and laborer. When John Ford tested him for the lead in his epic *Iron Horse* (1924), George was sharing a small apartment with Gary Cooper, Mervyn LeRoy, and Charles Farrell[2]. He was the first unknown lead in a major production, and it made him a star overnight. The film, which also starred Madge Bellamy (living in Ontario, California), was the year's box-office smash, and is still considered one of the truly classic examples of silent movies. He was placed under contract to William Fox with a starting salary of $125 a week and set right to work turning out one feature after another. He played opposite Dorothy Mackaill (still a friend of George's and living at the Royal Hawaiian Hotel in Honolulu) in *The Man Who Came Back* (1924), made *Thank You* (1925) with Jacqueline Logan (single and living in Melbourne Beach, Florida), *Honor Bound* (1928) with Leila Hyams (Mrs. Phil Berg of Bel Air, California), *True Heaven* (1929) with Lois Moran (Mrs. Clarence Young of Palo Alto, California), and *The Lone Star Ranger* (1930) with Sue Carol (the widow of Alan Ladd lives in Beverly Hills). He had been scheduled to do the original version of *Seventh Heaven* but was replaced by Charles Farrell and cast instead in *Sunrise* (1927), one of the greatest motion pictures ever made. His talkies were all big money-makers but they were not "A" products.

George was billed throughout most of his career as: "A man's man and the idol of women." Up until he returned to service during World War II he appeared in popular outdoor action features that he partly owned. George performed nearly all his own stunts in such pictures as *The Last Trail* (1933), with the late J. Carrol Naish, *Daniel Boone* (1936), with Heather Angel (her husband was murdered in 1969; she lives in Montecito, California), and *The Marshal of Mesa City* (1940), with Leon Ames (proprietor of a Ford dealership in Los Angeles). Since World War II he has appeared in only five movies and then only in featured roles such as in *She Wore a Yellow Ribbon* (1949) and *Cheyenne Autumn* (1964).

George O'Brien's private life was never really touched by his career, aside from the fact that he married Marguerite Churchill, his leading lady in *The Riders of the Purple Sage* (1931). His children never knew their dad was in movies until he took them to see one of his pictures. "We were so busy with the art of living on our ranch that the subject just never came up," George said recently. His daughter, Orin, was the first woman ever to play with the New York Philharmonic and his son, Darcy, is a teacher and an authority on James Joyce. The O'Briens were divorced in 1948 after fifteen years of marriage. Marguerite now resides in Lisbon, Portugal.

George is healthy, wealthy, and has total recall of his colorful life, which includes military duty with NATO and SHAPE. He maintains a beautiful home in Brentwood, California, but at a moment's notice will take off for Europe or the South Seas. Director John Ford, who gave him his big break in *Iron Horse*, is still one of his closest friends.

A longtime Hollywood observer said of him recently: "It's a pity that all of George's fans can't meet him because he's exactly the man they loved on the screen. A big, strong, thoroughly decent human being."

Today, next to an ad for "My Wild Irish Rose" (1947). *Alicia Rosineh*

Brett Morrison as Lamont Cranston, "distinguished young man about town."

THE SHADOW

The invisible man whose adventures enthralled radio listeners for twenty-four years began on CBS on August 31, 1930, on "Detective Story Hour." At first, The Shadow only hosted the program. The original role was played for the first few weeks by Jack LaCurto, who left to do a Broadway play, and Frank Readick took over. From September 6, 1931, to June 5, 1932, the show was called "Blue Coal Musical Revue." Blue Coal sponsored the program for most of the time it was on the air, and in later years featured their "distinguished heating expert," announcer John Barclay, in the commercials. "The Shadow" moved to NBC for the 1932–33 season and then returned to CBS where it stayed until March 27, 1935, when it went over to the Mutual Broadcasting Company. For most of its time on the air the program was heard over Mutual in the late afternoon on Sundays. It ran thirty minutes.

By 1935 The Shadow had emerged as the chief character in all the scripts. He was handsome, well educated, independently wealthy, and possessed what today would be called "cool." The radio character derived from the hero of the Walter Gibson novels—283 written under the name of Maxwell Grant. Gibson's publisher, Street and Smith, for years did a brisk business with The Shadow in the comics and the magazine of that name. In the comic books the character was always depicted in a large black hat and a high-collared cape. Although it was a well-kept secret at the time, Arch Oboler (now a Los Angeles resident) wrote many of the radio scripts under a pen name, and for less than his usual fee.

At the outset, the announcer would give the origin of The Shadow's powers—that during a trip to the Orient, Lamont Cranston, alias The Shadow, had learned "the power to cloud men's minds so that they could not see him." Featured in all the stories was The Shadow's "friend and companion, the lovely Margot Lane." The first actress to play the part of Margot, the only person who knew The Shadow's true identity, was Agnes Moorehead; Leslie Woods was the last actress in the role. Keenan Wynn originated the role of Shrevie. The third actor to play the title role was Robert Hardy Andrews, replaced by Orson Welles, replaced by Bill Johnstone. Bret Morrison, who got the part after doing a cold reading, stepped in as The Shadow in 1944 and stayed with it to the last broadcast at the close of December 1954. Even occasional listeners still remember Bret's opening lines (spoken through a filter) : "Who knows what evil lurks in the hearts of men? The Shadow knows! [*sinister sustained laugh*]," accompanied by Saint-Saëns's "Omphale's Spinning Wheel" on the organ. The tune also closed the program.

During the final decade of its run, "The Shadow" was broadcast before a live audience at the Longacre Theatre in New York City, except for the last four months of Grace Matthews's pregnancy when they moved into a studio rather than risk the audience reacting to their hero's then "faithful companion" being five months gone. The show's audience comprised as many adults as it did young people, although much of the fan mail indicated a remarkable lack of maturity. During times of war (WWII and the Korean War), many letters damned the producers for restricting the invisible man to home, where they felt he was wasting his time on small-fry crooks. Adolescent boys spent hours musing over what they would do if only they could not be seen by girls!

"The Shadow" was revived in the late sixties when the old recordings were syndicated around the country, and in late 1972 was again revived briefly on WRVR in New York.

Bret Morrison since leaving the show has made a successful career of dubbing foreign films into English. His company did most of the *Hercules* films, in which Morrison's voice (sans filter) was dubbed for many of the actors. In 1970 Bret, a widower, moved from Manhattan to Palm Springs, where he resides with his son.

After having performed in Broadway plays and feature films and in many other radio roles, including a stint as Mr. First Nighter, Bret is still constantly sought out for news of Lamont Cranston. Many of the kids glued to their radios those long-ago afternoons are now executives and producers Bret deals with almost daily. He reminds "Shadow" fans: "The weed of crime bears bitter fruit. Crime does not pay. The Shadow knows! [*sinister laugh*]."

The Shadow was visible recently in Manhattan. *Punkin Kohn*

Jane *(lower left)*, Patti *(center)*, and Helen *(right)* about 1934.

THE PICKENS SISTERS

Radio's singing trio were born in Macon, Georgia, in the order of Helen, Jane, and Patti. Jane was the most ambitious, studying music in Europe and at the Curtis Institute in Philadelphia. Their parents always loved music and encouraged the girls to sing. Even at pre-grammar-school age, the girls were entertaining audiences at parties and church socials.

In 1930, at a party in New York City, the late Stella Karns, Mary Margaret McBride's[3] manager, heard them sing. She referred them to NBC, which was looking for a sister act to replace the CBS-bound Boswell Sisters.[1] The girls made a record, which the network liked so much it signed them without an audition.

Before Patti had joined them, the original third Pickens girl was Grace, who had left the group shortly after they hit big. She married U.S. Attorney John Cahill and acted for a while as their manager. Grace, who today lives alone in Manhattan, was replaced by the late Marla Forbe. But Marla was with them only three months because an agent talked her into pursuing a career on her own. That was when Patti joined the girls, and they remained together until Jane replaced Gertrude Niesen in the *Ziegfeld Follies of 1936*. At that time the trio disbanded.

Before the Pickenses went on the air in 1931, radio listeners nationwide knew of them through the huge NBC publicity campaign to launch their program, which was heard at prime time. Along with their twice-daily program (the second broadcast had to be done for the West Coast) and guest appearances on shows like the "Maxwell House Show Boat," they sang for a while with the Buddy Rogers orchestra on the Park Sheraton Roof. At one point they were doing five shows a day at the Paramount Theatre with Eddie Duchin and two nightly at the Rockefeller Center Rainbow Room in addition to their radio work. Somehow they found time to make movie shorts like *Good Luck & Best Wishes* (1934), with Warren Hull (living in retirement in Virginia Beach, Virginia), and one feature, *Sitting Pretty* (1933), with Jack Oakie[2] and Jack Haley.[3] They made records but never had a hit. Even their theme, "Just You and I," wasn't a big seller.

After they broke up, Helen married wealthy stockbroker Thomas W. Acheson. The couple live on the twenty-fifth floor of a luxury condominium in Fort Lauderdale, Florida. Patti, who was always the girl in the center, married Robert Simmons, a tenor with the Revelers, heard on radio. Patti and Robert played the strawhat circuit and clubs, and in 1941 Patti took over for ailing Jane in the Broadway musical *Boys and Girls Together*. Robert died in 1960, and the following year Patti, who is retired, married the Reverend Charles Shreve, pastor of an Episcopal church in Murray Hill, New Jersey. One of the couple's closest friends is Gloria Swanson.

Jane continued on stage in *Regina* (1949), the musical version of *The Little Foxes*, and revived *Music in the Air* on the stage in 1951. In 1953 she had her own NBC television show. The next year she married Park Avenue multimillionaire William C. Langley. A familiar face on the New York social scene ever since, Jane, who is now a widow, for years produced and hosted the annual telethon for cerebral palsy. Last year she made an unsuccessful Republican bid for election to Congress from Manhattan's Eighteenth Silk Stocking district, Mayor Lindsay's original district.

The sisters, who keep in close touch, have not sung together since the mid-fifties when they appeared with Ed Sullivan on his Sunday night TV show.

Jane, a New York socialite and would-be politician.

Patti today. *Don Ratka*

Helen in her Florida condominium. *Michael Knowles*

In 1942.

GLORIA JEAN

The girl who was to replace Deanna Durbin—and didn't—was born Gloria Jean Schoonover on April 14, 1926, in Buffalo, New York. By the age of three she was making occasional singing appearances in vaudeville and radio in Scranton, Pennsylvania, where the family had settled. Her billing was "Baby Schoonover."

A string of bad breaks that plagued her continually throughout her career began with an illness when she was six years old, making it impossible for her to accept an offer to tour with Paul Whiteman. Nevertheless, she became so popular locally that at Scranton's Capitol Theatre she packed the house.

At thirteen, her teacher took her to New York to pursue an operatic career. But Joe Pasternak, Deanna Durbin's producer, heard her sing, and she was signed to a contract by Universal Pictures. The thinking on the lot was that since their biggest star, Deanna Durbin, was now ready for ingenue roles, Gloria could take over in the preteen parts.

Her debut, *The Under-Pup* (1939), although inexpensively made, was a perfect showcase for her, and was quite successful. Universal was convinced she had great potential. Her second, *If I had My Way* (1940), with Bing Crosby, was disappointing as a film but proved again that Gloria had a certain personal appeal and a lovely soprano voice. She made *Never Give a Sucker an Even Break* (1941) with W. C. Fields, who she remembers was very considerate of her, although she was disturbed by his nose; it reminded her of a melting popsicle.

It is remarkable that Gloria Jean ranks so high in popularity among old-movie buffs and still-collectors since she never was a major star. Her films were at best mediocre. Some of them are *What's Cooking?* (1942), with the Andrews Sisters,[3] *When Johnny Comes Marching Home* (1942), with Jane Frazee (now a Southern California real estate agent), *River Gang* (1945), *Copacabana* (1947), and *There's a Girl in My Heart* (1949), with Elyse

30

Knox (married to sportscaster Tom Harmon; their daughter is married to Rick Nelson).

What *didn't* happen in Gloria Jean's career is much more interesting. She turned in a memorable performance as the blind girl with the late Alan Curtis in *Destiny* (1944), but the picture, originally supposed to be the opening episode of *Flesh and Fantasy,* was instead released on its own, with footage added—hastily and cheaply shot. The following year her appearance at London's Casino was a critical disaster. Gloria, who had never experienced bad notices or an unappreciative audience, broke down on stage. A vaudeville tour scheduled to follow was cancelled and she returned to Hollywood very shaken and somewhat embittered. Gloria was seen a few times on television in the early fifties and by 1954 was reduced to starring in a poverty-row programmer entitled "Air Strike." The real heartbreak came when Jerry Lewis announced that she would make her comeback in his film *The Ladies' Man* (1961). She left her job as hostess at a restaurant across from Republic studios and was promised a big part and songs. In the print that was released she didn't even have a single line. It would have been her first color movie.

Gloria Jean shares a small house in Canoga Park, California, with her mother and sister and her son from an unsuccessful marriage. She works daily as a receptionist at a cosmetic firm in nearby Van Nuys.

In a recent interview the former star told how the people she had helped in Hollywood when she was on top had turned away when she needed them. "Bing Crosby once told me to stay close to my family," she said. "It's a good thing I did because they're all I have now." All the money she had saved during her peak years went for back taxes. About her future she commented: "I thought that making movies was going to be my life. I loved it so much and I'd just give anything to be able to work again, even in small parts, but I know I'm too heavy and my age is against me."

Recently, Sammy Davis, Jr., in a chance encounter with Gloria and her boy, nine-year-old Angelo Cellini, told her that the boy should model or act in pictures. Davis had no idea who the boy's mother was. "I just couldn't bring myself to tell him," Gloria said. "I've changed so much I was afraid of how he'd react."

On her afternoon relief at Redkin Cosmetics, Van Nuys, California. *Frank Tudisco*

In 1946.

JOHN LODER

The handsome leading man of British and Hollywood films was born on March 1, 1898, to General Sir William and Lady Frances Lowe. He spent his early boyhood in York and other garrison towns in England before being sent off to Eton at thirteen. The First World War interrupted an education at the Royal Military College when he left to serve as a second lieutenant at Gallipoli, making him the then youngest officer in the British army. He was captured and held in France. Afterward he served on the Upper Silesia Plebiscite Commission and other Allied bodies.

Alexander Korda, who liked John, gave him his new surname and a very small part in the German silent film *Madame Doesn't Want Children* (1927), which included unknown extra Marlene Dietrich.

John thereafter was signed to a Paramount contract and appeared in the studio's last silent western, *Sunset Pass* (1929), as well as their first all-talkie, *The Doctor's Secret* (1929).

John continued throughout his career to make pictures both in the United States and England. In his Hollywood films John was usually the second leading man, whereas in England he not only got the girl but was considered the industry's glamour boy. He made *Murder Will Out* (1930) with Lila Lee,[1] *The Seas Beneath* (1931), the classic *Private Lives of Henry VIII* (1933), *Java Head* (1935), with Elizabeth Allan (living in Patterson, New York), and *King Solomon's Mines* (1937), with Paul Robeson.[2] Many of his efforts were Bs, such as *Diamond Frontiers* (1940), with the late Anne Nagel, *The Gorilla Man* (1942), with Paul Cavanaugh (living in Los Angeles), and *The Brighton Strangler* (1945), with Rose Hobart (living in Los Angeles). The few really fine films he made in the latter part of his career were *How Green Was My Valley* (1941), *Now, Voyager* (1942), *Old Acquaintance* (1943), and *The Hairy Ape* (1944).

His marriage to Hedy Lamarr, then one of the most publicized stars in the world, on May 27, 1943, made front pages everywhere, but did little for his career. He appeared opposite Hedy in her own production of *Dishonored Lady* (1947) after they had separated, and only because his studio threatened him with suspension if he refused. She and Loder, who had been married previously to the French actress Micheline Cheirel, were divorced in 1948. They had two children, Denise and Anthony.

In 1947 John had the lead on Broadway in *For Love or Money*, which had Grace Kelly in a featured role.

In the last two decades John Loder has acted hardly at all. He was in *The Story of Esther Costello* (1957) and *Gideon of Scotland Yard* (1959), but most of his time has been spent pursuing the pleasures of an active private life. He has always been known as a great ladies' man. Anna Lee (married to novelist Robert Nathan and living in West Hollywood), who costarred with him a number of times, recently referred to him as "the most beautiful man I've ever seen."

He and second wife Evelyn Auffmordt ended their six-year marriage in 1955. His last wife, the owner of a huge ranch in Argentina, was a widow when he married her in 1958. The ever-increasing head of cattle he owns—latest count over 38,000—he records on a slip of paper in his wallet.

Much of his time is spent in London where he keeps a small flat on Eaton Place. When not being the man about town he is working on his autobiography, which was inspired by the success of David Niven's book. "I may not be as big a name as Niven," he told an interviewer, "but I promise you that I've more stories to tell and they're a damn sight juicer!"

Today, in his London apartment.
Joan Fiore

In *Whistling in Dixie* (1942), co-starring Red Skelton.

ANN RUTHERFORD

The actress best remembered for playing Andy Hardy's girl friend was born in Toronto, Canada, on November 2, 1920. Her father was a tenor at the Metropolitan Opera. Her mother, Lucille Mansfield, had played second lead in the Pearl White serials. Therese Ann Rutherford was in the first grade when her family moved to San Francisco. She performed in a number of plays there, and when she was eleven the family settled in Los Angeles.

One day, after being reprimanded by a teacher for reading Edna St. Vincent Millay in class instead of doing her assignment, Ann decided on a change of pace. She roller-skated to KFAC and auditioned for and got the title role in the radio series "Nancy and Dick in the Spirit of '76." It was sponsored by the D.A.R. Richard Quine (now a movie director) was featured in the role of Dick. She was on radio for several years, when an agent saw Ann's photo in the newspaper and took her to Mascot Films. She was put under contract, and debuted in *Waterfront Lady* (1935). Ann was Gene Autry's[1] leading lady in several features and she played opposite John Wayne in six westerns.

Shortly after Ann began making movies, Jack La Rue (retired and living in North Hollywood) and the late Grant Withers were pointed out to her. Both had been stars and were now doing featured parts in a B picture. When she asked how that could happen she was told that they hadn't saved their money and had to take whatever they could get. The incident so impressed her that even when she was making $500 a week, she rode the bus to the studio. When M-G-M, who signed her in 1937, threatened to drop her option if she did not forfeit the raise due her, she merely waved a fat bankbook at them and called their bluff.

Although she has been in seventy-three features, including *Gone With the Wind* (1939) and *Orchestra Wives* (1942), most fans know her for playing Polly in the famed "Hardy" series. She is pleased with the way it turned out, but originally she did not want the role. She remembers having to stand in a hole in scenes with Mickey Rooney, so she wouldn't look too much taller than him.

Her other movies include *Dancing Co-ed* (1939), with Richard Carlson (living in Malibu where he writes TV scripts), *Pride and Prejudice* (1940), *Happy Land* (1943), with Dickie Moore,[3] and *Whistling in Brooklyn* (1944). After leaving M-G-M in 1942, her only film of any importance was *The Secret Life of Walter Mitty* (1947). When Metro called her back for a role in *They Only Kill Their Masters* (1972), the last feature shot on the Culver City lot before it was demolished, it was her first picture in twenty-two years. Much of it was shot on the old Andy Hardy set just before it was razed to make way for a shopping center.

Ann did some TV during the 1950s, such as "Playhouse 90" and "Studio One," but now has very little interest in working. Her second husband, William Dozier, whom she married in 1953, asked her to guest on his "Batman" TV series, but she wouldn't. Her first marriage, for eleven years, was to department-store heir David May.

Ann lives in a big, white colonial house across the street from Debbie Reynolds' in Beverly Hills. Weekends are spent at the Dozier Malibu beach house. She and her husband, whose previous wife is Joan Fontaine, are very much part of the Hollywood social scene. Ann likes to make paper flowers and refinishes furniture, which she enjoys more than moviemaking. "I don't miss my profession because I'm married to a producer. I read all the trade papers and hear all the gossip, but now I'm more of it than in it and that's fine with me."

With two of her interests today, her poodles. *Ray Kozlowski*

John moved from M-G-M to Republic Pictures in 1942.

JOHN CARROLL

The Hollywood leading man was born Julian Lafay in New Orleans on July 17, 1905. He ran away from home in his early teens and worked his way around the world selling newspapers, working in a steel mill, and as a merchant seaman. Then he turned up in Hollywood as a stuntman in the early 1930s.

John Carroll's life reads like a screenplay except that if it were filmed, his acting was never good enough for him to play the lead. John began in action films under contract to R-K-O. Among his first were *Muss 'Em Up* (1936) and *We Who Are About to Die* (1936). He played cads, cutups, cowboys and caballeros. Occasionally he was required to put on a suit and tie to serve as a backdrop to female stars. Although he says he never made a good picture in his life, *A Letter for Evie* (1945) was good, as was *Only Angels Have Wings* (1939). However, his *Rose of the Rio Grande* (1938) is something of a classic for buffs who prize movies that are so bad they are entertaining.

Carroll was famous in Hollywood for blowing his lines, usually in language even today's permissiveness wouldn't allow. And for his outlandish conduct. Before he was a name he bought a white police dog and a white Duesenberg, hoping to get a date with Joan Crawford, which he didn't. In 1938, he was arrested and thrown into jail by mistake, but before leaving the jail he bailed out every vagrant in it.

He was put under contract to M-G-M as a threat to Clark Gable but the two became good friends. The woman who headed Metro's talent department tried her best to get Louis B. Mayer to drop Carroll (she found him completely talentless). She failed and has been his wife for over twenty years.

No one could understand why Carroll would want his release from prestigious M-G-M to go to Republic—until it was learned that he had negotiated a contract that paid him $7,000 a week. Carroll, who has also produced several mediocre pictures, including Ethel Barrymore's last, *Johnny Trouble* (1957), always had a reputation among Hollywoodites for being a soft touch and an amusing companion. When Marilyn Monroe had given up hope of a career in films and was about to take a job as a carhop at a drive-in, Carroll and his wife took her into their home. They put her under personal contract for $100 a week in 1947. Through him, she met Metro's Billy Grady, who gave her the part in *Asphalt Jungle* (1950).

John's acting credits include *Flying Tigers* (1942), *Fiesta* (1947), and *The Farmer Takes a Wife* (1953).

Carroll spent all the money he made during his heyday. But when the land boom came to the San Fernando Valley in the 1950s, he had a large ranch in Granada Hills to sell and, through manipulation and speculation in real estate, has become a millionaire. He has a big house in St. Petersburg, Florida, set along the Gulf of Mexico. Here outside his back door he docks his yacht. He has a collection of guns including the one that killed Billy the Kid and one that killed Russ Columbo. Another trophy is an autographed copy of *Mein Kampf* given him by Hitler when Carroll won an auto race in Berlin in 1937.

Always projecting a sureness that bordered on the foolhardy, he says: "I was always a bit on the frightened side. People tell me I came over looking just the opposite. I've only seen one of my pictures. That was enough. Boy, was I bad!"

Rich now, and living in St. Petersburg, Florida. *Anselma Dell'Olio*

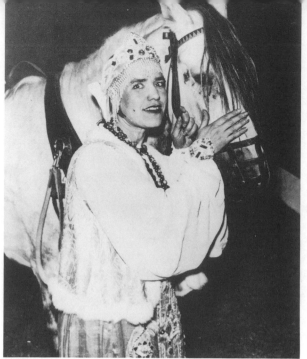

In 1932, doing an equestrian act with the Cirque d'Hiver in European capitals. *UPI*

MARIA RASPUTIN

The daughter of Russia's mad monk was born in 1898 in West Siberia. Her earliest recollections are of her father taking her to play with the Czar's children on the palace grounds in St. Petersburg. Maria claims that there was an endless flow of people who came to her father's apartment seeking his help and advice. She said recently that her father had always denied that he was holy, as people called him. "He was a religious man," she says, "but not a fanatic." She says, however, that she did witness Rasputin's healing of both humans and animals.

After the famous night of December 16, 1916, when the late Russian Prince Felix Yussoupov and several collaborators ferociously murdered Rasputin, the first of many changes in Maria's life began. When Lenin came to power with the crest of the Revolution, Maria's sister (who had worked in the Czarina's hospital), brother, and mother were sent to Siberia. Maria avoided arrest by the Bolshevists and made her way to Vladivostok. From there, in 1920 she left Russia forever.

Maria first landed in Berlin, where she made her living for a while as a Russian folk dancer. While touring the continent with her act, she met and married a White Russian officer, Boris Solovieff. By the time he died of tuberculosis, in 1927, Maria had begun to work with ponies and received an offer from a circus that hoped to capitalize on her maiden name. She had already sold her account of her father's gory death to a number of newspapers, including the *Boston Sunday Post*.

38

Maria found she had quite a way with animals and began to work with lions. That mastered, she added a half-dozen tigers to her act, which became quite a draw in Europe. She claimed to be able to hypnotize wild animals, but shortly after her arrival in the United States, in 1935, she was attacked by a Himalayan bear during a performance in Peru, Indiana. She required twelve stitches and five weeks in the hospital. After that she spent two seasons, beginning in 1937, headlining with the Barnum & Bailey Circus.

During World War II Maria worked as a shipfitter and then became a waitress in Los Angeles. Following the war, in 1946, she divorced her second husband, Gregory Bern, an engineer. They have two daughters and eight grandchildren.

Maria Gregorievna Rasputin's life is still overshadowed by her father. She lives in a small house in a White Russian neighborhood in Los Angeles, near the Russian Orthodox church where she worships. The priests and congregation are very aware that she is Rasputin's daughter, as are the inhabitants of the Russian Old People's Home where she helps out a few days a week. Most of the students who come to her for Russian lessons first became aware of her as Rasputin's daughter.

For two years now, with the help of a journalist, Maria has been working on a book entitled "Rasputin's Secret Diaries."

Maria told a journalist recently that her father would be understood by young people today, more so than he was by his Russian contemporaries. "He warned the Czar over and over not to make war," she said. "They say he was a spy. He was God's spy." She tells about his playing with her one day when he threw a ball into the air so high it disappeared. When she asked where it went, Rasputin replied: "God caught it."

In front of her father's picture in her Los Angeles home. *Jos. O'Donohue IV*

In 1946 Shirley Temple and John were the most popular newlyweds in America.

JOHN AGAR

The actor who became famous as Shirley Temple's husband (her first) was born in Chicago on January 21, 1921. His father headed the family-owned meat-packing company. While John was in the army (an Air Force sergeant) he was a house guest of his mother's friend ZaSu Pitts. The former star's next-door neighbor, Shirley Temple, asked John to take her to a party hosted by her boss, David O. Selznick. At the party, the producer felt Agar out about an acting career, and after John's army discharge he was put under contract.

When Shirley Temple became Mrs. John Agar, in 1946, they announced they would manage on his earnings—then $150 a week—save all of hers, and move into what had been her dollhouse on her parents' property. The Agars were surely the most popular couple in America.

John made his debut in *Fort Apache* (1948) with his wife, and they were again teamed in *Adventure in Baltimore* (1949). But almost from the beginning of their marriage, rumors of discord filtered through Hollywood and into the press. The overnight success and the inevitable title of "Mr. Shirley Temple" set Agar off on a drinking spree that brought them to a bitter divorce in 1949.

John stayed with Selznick for five years, although all his films, such as *She Wore a Yellow Ribbon* (1949) and *Breakthrough* (1950), were made on loan-out. His divorce didn't stop his career, but neither did it slow his drinking. By 1951 his numerous arrests for drunk driving brought him sixty days on a prison farm. In May, 1951, a judge refused to marry him to his present wife until he drank enough black coffee to be sober for the ceremony. Two years later he was arrested twice in one day and drew a four-month sentence.

In 1954 John made three features, including *Shield for Murder*. He then began making low-budget science-fiction and horror movies, almost an irreversible course to oblivion in Hollywood. *Revenge of the Creature* (1955) helped. He still turns up occasionally in a cheapie—*Young Fury* (1965)—or in a bit part—*Chisum* (1970).

John tried a number of business ventures without much success. He attempted to form a lecture bureau which offered movie stars and briefly operated a chain of cotton candy concessions.

Today he is a very sober insurance salesman in the San Fernando Valley near his home in Burbank. The Agars live with their two sons, two dogs, a rabbit, a mouse, a goldfish, and his ninety-year-old father-in-law.

What of his continuing his acting career? "I never made a movie that pleased me but living has given me more dimension than I had then. I simply wasn't ready when it was handed to me. Yes, I'd really like another shot at it."

He speaks well of his ex-wife but they have no contact. When asked about their daughter, now in her mid-twenties, all John is certain of is that she is not married.

Now an insurance salesman. *Kendra Kerr*

SHERRY BRITTON

The stripper who became the star performer of New York's long-gone Leon & Eddie's supper club was born Edith Britton on July 23, 1924, in New Brunswick, New Jersey. When she was two and one-half years old, her parents were divorced and she was placed in an orphanage; after that she was a foster child transferred from one couple to another. She can remember at least sixteen different addresses during those years but recalls there were many more.

In 1937 she changed her name to Sherry, which she took from a bottle of Harvey's Bristol Cream, thus becoming, according to her, the world's first Sherry. In those days she was put up by various girl friends.

An agent suggested she audition for burlesque, and she landed her first job in the chorus at the People's Theatre on the Bowery. After a week she was a principal. In her debut as a single, at the age of thirteen, Sherry had the bust of a well-built twenty-year old, a Shirley Temple hairdo, and a missing tooth. The audience roared when they saw her breasts, and Sherry panicked and fainted.

For five years, she traveled around the country on various burlesque wheels, hating every minute of what she calls a dreadful atmosphere. On Christmas Day, 1937, in a theatre raid, she was arrested in Burbank, California. But the police didn't know how young she was. She was put on probation and then went directly to San Francisco to strip some more. Without a manager and no business sense of her own, Sherry was exploited by theatre after theatre. Although she and Margie Hart (now residing in Beverly Hills, California) were the top two burlesque queens among New York audiences, the highest salary Sherry ever made—at Minsky's—was $75 a week.

"Stripping always bothered me," she said recently. "I've always considered myself amoral, but the cheapness of burlesque and the disrespect the people seemed to have for me and themselves in that business troubled me a great deal."

Things changed with the outbreak of World War II. Sherry went to Leon & Eddie's where she remained for seven and a half years as the headliner. Though the club, too, was raucous, Sherry stripped for big-name patrons— and for a very large salary. Pinups of her were so popular among U.S. servicemen that President Roosevelt made her an honorary Brigadier General for "keeping up the morale of our boys."

After leaving Leon & Eddie's, Sherry played top clubs in major cities, during the winter months, and appeared on the strawhat circuit in summers for very substantial fees. Although she has never appeared on Broadway, Sherry has been in forty-eight legitimate shows, such as road companies of *Getting Gertie's Garter* (1942), *Peer Gynt* (1951) with John Garfield, and *Oklahoma!* (1959) with Harold Lang (now teaching at a college in Daly City, California). Her marriage to a singer she met while starring in *Bus Stop* in 1955 was annulled in 1958.

Her *Best of Burlesque* show, which she did with Tom Poston at the Carnegie Hall Playhouse in 1957, and the record album taken from it, is believed by many in show business to have inspired *This Was Burlesque*. This was stripper Ann Corio's show which made several million dollars during the 1960s. "I'm happy that Ann did so well," says Sherry, "but I think she could be a little more gracious about me when people bring the subject up."

In 1971, the former Queen of the Undress Circle married her boyfriend of ten years, Robert Gross, the president and chairman of Astra Aircraft. They share a large apartment on Manhattan's Gramercy Park.

Sherry had been in analysis for nine years and feels she would like to be a therapist, and says: "I'm over all the mental agony caused by those years stripping in filthy bump and grind houses. But when people ask me if there wasn't anything I enjoyed about it I have to admit that stopping a show, which I did more than a few times, is the closest thing to an orgasm I've ever experienced. Considering how empty and lonely my personal life was back then I guess it was a substitute. Maybe I was a sex goddess to a lot of guys but while they were fantasizing, Sherry was going home at 4 A.M. alone, lonely and tired."

On the walls of U.S. Armed Forces barracks around the world during WWII.

Today Mrs. Sherry Britton-Gross of Gramercy Park. *Tim Boxer*

No one could look quite so stupid.

ALLEN JENKINS

The character actor who epitomizes the dumb hoodlum was born Al McGonegal on Staten Island in 1900. Although his parents were show people his only interest was marine architecture—until he worked for a summer as an assistant stage manager in a Broadway show. He was given a scholarship at the American Academy of Dramatic Arts, where his father was an instructor.

He and his roommate, Jimmy Cagney, were chorus boys in *Pitter-Patter* (1920). In 1923, Allen played a Marine and understudied the lead in the national company of *Rain,* which toured the United States for fifty-seven weeks. He appeared in a bit part and doubled as assistant stage manager on *Secrets* (1924). His combined salary was $40 a week. A friendship with Pat O'Brien (living in Brentwood, California) began in 1927 when they went on the road in *Broadway.* In it, Jenkins played a gangster. He was killed during the first act. In *The Last Mile* (1930), he was a convicted murderer and took over the lead when Spencer Tracy left to make a movie.

Jenkins's real break came when he got the part of Frankie Wells in *Blessed Event,* a Broadway hit of 1932 starring Roger Pryor. Jenkins gave audiences their first look at the gangster-as-near-moron, who couldn't be trusted to hold a machine gun. He modeled his characterization on Goopie, a classmate of his from seventh-grade days whom he describes as "an embryo hoodlum." When Warner Brothers brought him to Hollywood to re-create the role in the film version (1932), he stole the picture and the notices.

In the next seven years, Jenkins put in what he calls "murderous hours" making seventy-seven features and five shorts. He and his pals under contract to the lot—Cagney, Pat O'Brien, William Gargan (living in Rancho

La Costa, California), and Frank McHugh (living in Cos Cob, Connecticut)—were known at Warner's as the Irish Mafia.

When Jenkins left in 1939, he was making $1,750 a week. He had played thugs, cab drivers, bartenders, body guards, and cops in such pictures as *42nd Street* (1933), *The Whirlpool* (1933), with Lila Lee,[1] *Broadway Hostess* (1935), with Wini Shaw (Mrs. Bill O'Malley of Sunnyside, Queens, New York), *The Singing Kid* (1936), with Beverly Roberts (now head of Theatre Authority in New York City), *Dance, Charlie, Dance* (1937), with Jean Muir (the blacklisted actress is now head of the Theatre Department of Stephens College in Missouri), *Heart of the North* (1938), with Dick Foran (living in Van Nuys, California), his favorite, the hilarious *A Slight Case of Murder* (1938), *A Date With the Falcon* (1941), with Wendy Barrie (residing in Manhattan), *Eyes in the Night* (1942), with Ann Harding (living in Westport, Connecticut), and *Wonder Man* (1945), with Virginia Mayo (married to Michael O'Shea and living in the San Fernando Valley).

In 1943, he was with Ethel Merman on Broadway in *Something for the Boys*. But not long afterward, a newspaper reported that he was working as a tool-and-die-maker at Douglas Aircraft for $89.50 a week. In 1952 he was selling cars. Seven years later he was appearing in *Hole in the Head* around the country, with Ann Corio, and has since been seen in various cities in *Lullaby* and *Kiss Me Kate*. His entrance never fails to bring a round of applause from the audience, many of whom don't remember his name but instantly recognize the hooked nose and Damon Runyonesque voice.

Allen is divorced from the childhood sweetheart he married in 1933 and lives alone in a senior citizen apartment house overlooking the Pacific Ocean in Santa Monica. Although bad investments have taken much of the money he made during his youth, he lives very comfortably and is in excellent health, since he gave up drinking and smoking completely. He recently did a role on "Marcus Welby, M.D.", and is considering opening a little theatre in Carmel, California.

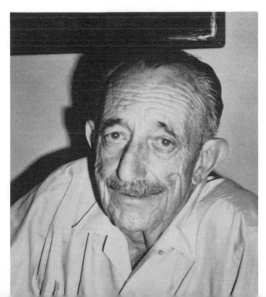

Today, in his apartment overlooking the Pacific. *Michael Knowles*

A rare shot of Virginia smiling.

VIRGINIA O'BRIEN

The deadpan singer-comedienne was born on April 18, 1921. Her father was captain of detectives of the Los Angeles police department for twenty-two years before spending fifteen years as prosecuting attorney. Although she never had any professional aspirations, she began taking dancing lessons after seeing Eleanor Powell[2] in several movies. But since she was frail, her family prevailed upon her to switch to singing.

One of the producers of "Meet the People" heard her practice and suggested she audition for the show, which was about to open in Los Angeles; the director liked her imitation of Ethel Merman. She was cast in the production, but when she went on stage opening night she froze. Though she remembered every word of her song, she was unable to move a muscle. The audience was convulsed, but Virginia was in tears when she reached her dressing room. The producers consoled her with the news that though she didn't turn out the way anyone had planned, it was fine as far as they and the audience were concerned—and Louis B. Mayer. He had seen her number and after a test she was signed to an M-G-M contract.

Because of her uncle, the director Lloyd Bacon, Virginia wasn't as impressed with the stars she met at the Culver City lot as most teen-age girls might have been. But she did want to date some of the young men there, Robert Sterling, for one. However, word was passed that Mayer was a personal friend of her father's and that he took a special interest in her well-being.

And so John Raitt was the only one who ever asked her out. She married Kirk Alyn (Superman in the movies and now living in Los Angeles), who resented the greater publicity and attention given her.

The tall gal with the deadpan went over big with audiences of the 1940s and she could command as much as $5,000 a week for personal appearances in presentation houses. Some of her songs were "Rock-a-Bye, Baby" in *The Big Store* (1941), "Salome" in *Du Barry Was a Lady* (1943), "Take it Easy" in *Two Girls and a Sailor* (1944), and "Life upon the Wicked Stage" in *Till the Clouds Roll By* (1946). All were done with the stiff gestures and flat voice. The only time she remembers smiling was at the conclusion of her number in *Thousands Cheer* (1943).

Virginia was very happy at Metro but only in very few of her sixteen features did she ever do much more than her famous comedy songs. Her pleadings with the front office for other roles were ignored. By 1949 when Metro failed to pick up her option she was hopelessly typecast. The only movie work she was able to find thereafter was *Francis in the Navy* (1955), the year of her divorce. Virginia has worked off and on over the years in small clubs and although she has tried everything from country to Latin music, audiences want most to see her old routines. However, in her movies shown on TV, since sometimes her bits had been shot and added after completion of a picture, they are unessential to the plot and often are cut.

Virginia, who speaks with an unaccountable pronounced Texas drawl, travels a great deal with her present husband, contractor Harry B. White, in their small plane. They live with two of her four children in Encino, California; her daughter Terri from her first marriage has an all-girl rock band, The Cover Girls.

Virginia, still minus the famous deadpan, with her youngest child. *Michael Knowles*

With Senator Joseph McCarthy (*left*) in an exchange the public never saw, 1954. *UPI*

ROBERT T. STEVENS

The Secretary of the Army, who became the pivotal figure in the public clash that brought down Senator Joseph McCarthy, was born in Fanwood, New Jersey, on July 13, 1899. Robert Ten Broeck Stevens's father headed up the family firm of J. P. Stevens & Co., Inc., the multimillion-dollar textile concern. After graduating from Phillips Andover in 1917 and then Yale in 1921, he served in the Field Artillery in World War I. When the elder Stevens died in 1929, Robert took over as president of the family firm.

During FDR's first term, Stevens was on the staff of the National Recovery Administration and in 1940 headed up the textile section of the National Defense Advertising Commission. Later, in the Eisenhower days, he was rewarded for his early support and large contributions to Eisenhower's campaign by being named Secretary of the Army, in 1953.

In the spring of 1954, the late Senator Joseph McCarthy publicly attacked Pentagon officials and Army officers who, he suggested, were "coddling Communists." McCarthy was then at the crest of public support for his investigations.

Stevens, whose temperament and attitude were exactly opposite the senator's, was naturally inclined to ignore the accusations. But the attacks became so brutal that he felt forced to defend his department, in open Senate subcommittee hearings, which were televised live coast to coast. Among other things, the hearings catapulted one obscure individual to fame overnight. That was Army dentist Dr. Irving Peress (now practicing on Manhattan's West 57th Street) whose loyalty and promotion McCarthy felt were highly questionable. McCarthy denounced General Ralph Zwicker (now a retired brigadier general in Falls Church, Virginia) as "not fit to wear that uniform." The Army countercharged that McCarthy's aide, counsel Roy Cohn, had brought pressure on the Army to promote Cohn's rich buddy, Private G. David Schine (now active in motion picture production). Even a special counsel to the Senate subcommittee, Ray H. Jenkins,[1] wasn't able to control the Wisconsin senator.

McCarthy ran roughshod over Stevens, whose slow speech and hesitant manner made him seem weak, or guilty, rather than thoughtful. But after thirty-six days, twenty-two witnesses, and over two million words of testimony and verbal exchanges that became known as the Army-McCarthy hearings, the most powerful member of the Senate was exhausted—and he had been exposed to the American public as being devoid of fair play and emotional stability. The proceedings started out to try the Army and convicted McCarthy.

When Stevens left government service it was to return to his business and family. He has since turned over the presidency of the family firm to his second son, but remains chairman of the firm's executive committee. He is on the boards of such corporations as General Electric, General Foods, and Owens-Corning Fiberglas. He commutes several days a week to Manhattan from his large home in Edison, New Jersey, which he occupies with his wife, Dorothy, whom he married in 1923. The couple spend a lot of time on their 10,000-acre cattle ranch in Montana. Stevens is particularly fond of horseback riding.

Stevens, who is a great believer in military solutions to problems, has never fought in a war, has never been drafted, has never held rank below officer level, feels that President Nixon has made a great mistake in ending the draft. He dismisses the reports of low morale and widespread use of heroin among U.S. forces in Southeast Asia as gross exaggerations.

Still Chairman of the Board of the family firm. *Newsweek— Tony Rollo*

In *The Chocolate Soldier* (1941), her screen debut with Nelson Eddy.

RISË STEVENS

The mezzo-soprano was born Risë Steenberg in New York City, of American-Norwegian parentage. Her parents encouraged her early interest in music and by the time she was ten, teachers were telling them that she showed great promise. For several years, she sang on WJZ's "Children's Hour," where she met Milton Cross, its announcer.

Until vocal coach Mme Anna Schoen-Rene heard her and offered her a scholarship at Juilliard, Risë had not even considered opera. She was interested exclusively in Broadway. Years later, after becoming a star in opera, she turned down several Broadway starring offers.

The first time the Metropolitan offered her a contract, she declined it, choosing instead to gain more experience singing in Europe. Her debut in *Mignon* at the Prague Opera House in 1936 was a great success. She remained there for two years singing more than twenty-five roles.

Risë Stevens made her debut under the Metropolitan's auspices in Philadelphia on November 22, 1938, in *Der Rosenkavalier*. She was first heard in the Metropolitan Opera House itself on December 17, 1938, as Mignon.

Risë brought to opera not only a well-trained and beautiful voice, but she had a personal warmth and chic often lacking in prima donnas. That she was a very good actress and an American added greatly to her popularity. Among her colleagues, her discipline and unpretentiousness made her very well liked.

From her repertoire of more than forty roles she became the outstanding Octavian in *Der Rosenkavalier,* Delilah in *Samson and Delilah,* Orfeo, Hansel in *Hansel and Gretel,* and Carmen, to which she gave a sensuality that opera audiences had never seen before. She appeared in most of the world's great opera houses, like the Vienna State Opera, Teatro Colon in Buenos Aires, the Paris Opera, many international festivals, like Glyndebourne, the Athens festival, and at Milan's La Scala, where she became the first American to world-premiere an Italian opera, Virgilio Mortari's *La*

Figlia del Diavolo. The only two disappointments of her enviable career were that she never managed to sing with the tenor she admired so much, the late Jussi Bjoerling, and that *Tosca* was not within her vocal range.

Nelson Eddy asked M-G-M for her when Jeanette MacDonald turned down *The Chocolate Soldier* (1941). Although the picture was a critical and financial success, Risë didn't like the medium and found the Hollywood scene quite false. She refused to do *The Cat and the Fiddle,* and her contract was voided. Risë thoroughly enjoyed working with Bing Crosby, however, in *Going My Way* (1944), but thought her last film, *Carnegie Hall,* was dreadful.

On March 17, 1960, after a particularly good performance of *Rosenkavalier,* she calmly announced to husband, Walter Surovy, who was also her personal manager, and to Rudolf Bing, that she had sung her last at the Metropolitan. Surovy argued, Bing refused to believe her, but Risë would not even consent to give the traditional farewell performance. Years before she had seen Lucrezia Bori leave at the height of her career and vowed to do the same.

After a successful but limited run in Richard Rodgers' *The King and I,* which inaugurated the first musical theatre season at Lincoln Center's State Theater (one of the musicals she had originally turned down on Broadway), she served as the co-general manager of the Metropolitan's National Company, which existed for two years but had to be closed because the parent company could no longer finance it. The Surovys then retired to St. Thomas but several years ago moved back to Manhattan, where they occupy a large, glamorous apartment on the East Side. Their son, Nicholas, is an actor.

Her recordings are still selling briskly and fans often see her at plays and opera performances, but Risë doesn't see many people from the old days. In a recent and rare interview, she admitted that now and then she loves getting together with cronies. But most of her friends have nothing to do with entertainment, "except that", says Risë, "they are very entertaining." She is a board member of the National Council on the Arts and of the Metropolitan Opera Guild.

Very chic in her Manhattan apartment.
Michael Knowles

With Ella Raines in *Singing Guns* (1950).

VAUGHN MONROE

The singing idol and bandleader of the forties and fifties was born on October 7, 1911, in Akron, Ohio. At the age of fourteen Vaughn won a state trumpet contest. After graduating from high school in Jeannette, Pennsylvania, he enrolled at Carnegie Tech where he majored in voice, but he left college in 1933 to join a band. When the band broke up in 1935 he went with Larry Funk's group as a trumpeter and vocalist. After a year Jack Marshard offered Monroe the leadership of his band. The arrangement worked well for four years, but in 1940 Vaughn formed his own band and Marshard went with him as manager. Also that year, he played the Paramount Theatre for the first time, made his radio debut, and married his childhood sweetheart, Marian Baughman.

By the time Vaughn Monroe played Meadowbrook in the spring of 1941 he was well on his way to making it very big. In less than a year the country's top disc jockey, the late Martin Block, placed Monroe's band among the top twenty in his WNEW poll. He also had his own radio show in the forties and began making appearances in such films as *Meet the People* (1944) and *Carnegie Hall* (1947). And his band continued for ten years to roll up attendance records at the country's top spots, including New York's Commodore Hotel and Strand Theatre. Vaughn was the first to record "There, I've Said It Again," which has sold over 2½ million records. The second biggest hit in his career is "Ghost Riders in the Sky," a 4½ million seller. One of the recording industry's all-time successes is the Vaughn Monroe vocal of "Ballerina," which has just passed the 5 million mark. The one hit he didn't have—because he turned it down—was the perennial best-seller "Rudolph the Red-Nosed Reindeer."

Although the Monroe aggregation developed into quite a good band, its leader was the main attraction. Vaughn's big, deep baritone drew not only bobby-soxers but young married women, and more than a few matrons. But not everyone dug Monroe. Detroit's most popular disc jockey, Jack the Bellboy, made jokes about his squareness and pomposity daily, but he played his records just the same. No real personality was ever revealed by Monroe in his performances, and in his interviews he never drops the professional image, answering all questions with the pronoun *we*.

Vaughn has starred in two Republic westerns, *Singing Guns* (1950) and *Toughest Man in Arizona* (1952), and appeared with his band on CBS-TV from October 1950 to July 1951. They were back on NBC-TV for a short period in 1954.

In 1953 the Monroe entourage disbanded, including the Moonmaids, a female singing group, and he set out as a single. The band business had been slipping and he wanted to spend more time with his wife and two daughters. Along with playing clubs, for several years Vaughn acted as TV spokesman for RCA products on the company's TV commercials—a very lucrative venture for him. In 1967 he played the Rainbow Grill in Manhattan and in 1970 was featured at the St. Regis. He still commands a sizable fee for private parties but admits his audiences are made up of "those who remember, not the kids."

Vaughn, who lives in Jensen Beach, Florida, can well afford to spend most of his time sailfishing and playing golf. He has a solid marriage and several gold records that have earned a great deal of money. But his original goal, grand opera, has always eluded him. He seems to have little interest in popular music or performers and admits that after all these years in the business he has not made any close show biz friends. "We had some good friends among the bookers, though," he allowed during a recent radio interview.

At an interview with Michael Knowles during Vaughn's recent trip to Manhattan. *Ronnie Britton*

In 1952, when her unique voice was known all over the world. *NBC*

YMA SUMAC

The Nightingale of the Andes was born on September 10, 1927, in Ichocan, a small town in the mountains north of Lima, Peru. Her Spanish name is Emperatriz Chavarri. Yma Sumac, her Indian name, means "how beautiful."

She began singing locally at church festivals, but it was not until 1941 that a government official heard her extraordinary voice. She was then presented in a concert in Lima. Moises Vivanco, a musician and executive with the Peruvian Broadcasting Company, heard her and took over management of her career.

On June 6, 1942, Yma and Vivanco were married, and she became part of his Inca Taky Trio, which toured South America and Mexico before arriving in 1946 in the United States. Contrary to Vivanco's expectations, his wife was not an immediate success. Those who heard her low contralto, which has a range to A above high C, were impressed, but no one knew quite how this very unusual artist should be presented. Furthermore, Vivanco's very definite ideas about her repertory, arrangements, and publicity turned off several promoters. Yma recalls the four lean years she and her husband spent trying to make it in New York. They were very difficult years financially, and in the end results were disappointing; she feels that she had to compromise to be accepted. Yma was playing the now-defunct Blue Angel nightclub in New York when Capitol Records decided to take a chance with her and Vivanco. Her first album, which was produced by Alan Livingston, was released in 1950 with a publicity campaign that had her an Incan princess. The claim was soon contradicted, but *Voice of Xtabuy* went right onto the best-seller charts. *Mambo* and *Legend of the Sun Virgins* were also successful, and Yma, wearing exotic jewelry and clothes, began packing them in at such places as the Hollywood Bowl and New York's Hotel Pierre. She played an Arabian princess in the Broadway musical *Flahooley* in 1951 and in Hollywood made *Secret of the Incas* (1954) and *Omar Khayyam* (1957).

Then her private life began to get more newspaper space than her notices. In 1957 her husband lost a paternity suit brought by Yma's secretary, who had given birth to twins. Yma sued for a divorce but before it was granted, in 1958, the husband-wife-mistress confrontation, complete with hair-pulling, bruises, and a black eye, broke nationally. A year later the Vivancos were considering remarrying—all the while a private detective was suing Yma for nonpayment of a $1,180.22 bill for shadowing her husband before the divorce.

Yma toured Europe in the sixties and little was heard of her in the United States. She launched an attempted comeback in 1968, but it didn't materialize. A California concert was particularly disappointing.

For Miracles, her first album in thirteen years, she sang rock and roll. The 1972 release was not a success. Furthermore, Yma was extremely unhappy about the liner notes that credited Les Baxter with her early success. She plans next to record an album of country-and-western music.

Yma has never remarried and lives with her brother in San Francisco. Her son, Charles, is in college in Spain, where his father lives.

A recurring rumor about the artist with the five-octave voice is that she is a girl from Brooklyn named Amy Camus who decided to spell her name backwards. It is doubtful that anyone who has ever spoken with her went away believing it. Her English is like a parody of Carmen Miranda.

Yma now wants to sing country and western music.

A strong but limited appeal.

JOHN DEREK

Hollywood's pretty boy of the fifties was born Derec Harris in Los Angeles in 1926 to sometime actress Delores Johnson. His father was writer-director-actor Lawson Harris. By the time Derek was five years old, his parents were divorced. Cameraman Russell Harlan became John's father figure; he taught the boy to ride and swim, but this didn't overcome his fierce possessive attitude toward his mother. Even when his father took John to live with him during one of his flush periods (he was always either rolling in money or broke), John would visit his mother every day after school.

Both parents were contemptuous of acting. "I was brought up to think of acting as a girl's profession, like playing with dolls," says John today.

He admits to being terribly spoiled, but Hollywood completed the job. As a teen-ager, he was put under contract to David O. Selznick, and though he spent a year drawing $200 a week he never even bothered to show up for his acting lessons.

Derek spent 1945–46 in the army as a paratrooper and made sixteen jumps. When he was discharged, Twentieth Century-Fox signed him but his attitude was the same, and he left after a year.

Columbia gave him a contract and showcased him in *Knock on Any Door* (1949), with Humphrey Bogart. The fan magazines proclaimed him a star before the picture was even released and announced it as his debut even though he had made brief appearances in *Since You Went Away* (1944) and *I'll Be Seeing You* (1944). No sooner was the movie in the theatres than the studio received the biggest deluge of mail in its history. Columbia, however, realized that although Derek had great appeal, it was limited to young girls and homosexuals and put him into a series of action pictures, such as *Mask of the Avenger* (1951) and *The Adventures of Hajji Baba* (1954). He is embarrassed at the way he looked in those days.

Throughout his career John never complained about his parts. "My favorite part would have been no part at all," he says. "I was interested in girls, horseback riding, and cars. The only thing the movies ever had for me was money. I was cast on the basis of my looks and that was just fine with me because as long as I presented my body before the cameras I got paid."

It was just as well, because he showed up on screen in absurd costumes, mouthing foolish dialogue in such Saturday afternoon fare as *The Leather Saint* (1956), *Omar Khayyam* (1957), with Debra Paget (married to the nephew of Mme Chiang Kai-shek and living in Houston where he is the Counsel General for the Republic of Formosa), and *Prisoner of the Volga* (1960). But oddly enough, he gave one of the only good performances in *The Ten Commandments* (1956), and was perfectly satisfactory in *Prince of Players* (1955) and *Exodus* (1960), although he is fond of saying that he cannot and will not take direction.

During his five-year marriage to Patti Behrs, which ended in a 1955 divorce, he fathered a son and daughter. Two years later he married the then unknown Ursula Andress. Derek is an excellent still photographer and his pictures of his wife were certainly a great help to her in achieving stardom.

John has not acted in over a decade and swears that he never will again. He has directed several low-budget features, a few of which have never even been released. Only one, *A Boy . . . A Girl* (1969), with Dino Martin, got any notices, and they were uniformly negative. He is determined to continue, but admits that he doesn't get on well with the financiers, technicians, or actors—"I've been told I'm pretty offensive on a set, and I can believe it." His distaste for glamour notwithstanding, his Encino, California, home—complete with waterfall, an Excalibur automobile, fur rugs, and animal-hide tabletops—houses beautiful blonde TV actress Linda Evens, whom he refers to as "my love."

The director in his Encino, California, home. *J. Nicolesco-Dorobantzou*

Best Supporting Actress for her performance in *The Great Lie* (1941).

MARY ASTOR

The durable, brilliant star was born Lucile Vasconcells Langhanke on May 3, 1906, in Quincy, Illinois. Her mother deeply resented her and her father used her ruthlessly for the money and reflected glory that her career brought him.

While a teen-ager, after being tested and rejected by D. W. Griffith, she began getting bit parts in such silent pictures as *Sentimental Tommy* (1921) and *Bought and Paid For* (1922).

She moved from Tri-Art to Famous Players studios, doing featured roles and shorts. But it was *Beau Brummel* (1924) that changed her career—and her personal life. Its star, John Barrymore, had requested her for his leading lady and soon became her first lover. They were together again in *Don Juan* (1926). Publicized as "the cameo beauty," she made *Rose of the Golden West* (1927) and *Dressed to Kill* (1928). At that point, William Fox was paying her $3,750 a week, but her option was dropped because the studio felt she was unsuitable for talkies.

Her appearance in the play *Among the Married* proved what a good voice she had and Mary began moving about on a free-lance basis, concerning herself more with parts and salaries than with billing. She appeared in *Holiday* (1930), *Red Dust* (1932), and *Straight from the Heart* (1935), with Baby Jane Quigley (living in Berwyn, Pa.).

Then in 1936 during a custody fight with her second husband, Dr. Franklin Thorpe, over their daughter, newspapers began publishing what were purported to be pages from her diary that detailed Mary's affair with author George F. Kaufman. In her autobiography, *My Story* (1959), Mary explained that most of the pages they ran were forged. One disclosure, however, that she disliked acting and hated Hollywood, was never denied.

But in spite of the exposure, which was the Hollywood scandal of the decade, audiences burst into applause at her appearance in *Dodsworth* (1936), and the next year she was in *The Prisoner of Zenda* and *The Hurricane*—A features, with A-plus performances by Miss Astor. Mary was delightfully bitchy in *Midnight* (1939) and stole *The Great Lie* (1941) from Bette Davis, who was delighted when Mary took the Best Supporting Academy Award as well. Her contribution to *The Maltese Falcon* (1941) helped make it the motion-picture classic it is. After giving a delicious comic portrayal in *Palm Beach Story* (1942), she appeared in the films *Claudia and David* (1946), *Little Women* (1949), *A Kiss Before Dying* (1956), and *Return to Peyton Place* (1961). Her swan song came in *Hush . . . Hush, Sweet Charlotte* (1965).

During her infrequent but memorable appearances in the fifties, the television generation discovered her talents, notably in the role of Norma Desmond in *Sunset Boulevard*.

Mary Astor on screen, stage, and radio was versatile, beautiful, chic, and a splendid actress. As a human being she was less successful. She survived the movie switch to sound but at the same time lost her first husband, director Kenneth Hawks, in 1930 in a plane crash. Also, she almost lost the custody of her daughter, attempted suicide, conquered alcoholism, had an abortion, converted to Catholicism, and went through three divorces from men who, she complained, wanted only her money. She says that at the height of her fame she was "sick, spoiled, and selfish, prowling like some animal seeking momentary satisfaction. Sexually I was out of control."

She lives alone in an apartment overlooking the Pacific Ocean. A severe heart ailment limits her activity to viewing television, reading, and writing. She has produced two autobiographies and five novels. Her old movies on TV prove what buffs have long maintained—that Mary Astor is a flawless actress and a distinctive star second to none.

With her full-size Oscar that the Academy recently gave her to replace her 1941 statuette. *Academy of Motion Picture Arts & Sciences*

One of Hollywood's leading juvenile actors in the early 1940s.

JIMMY LYDON

The "Henry Aldrich" of the movies was born May 30, 1923, in Harrington Park, New Jersey, one of nine children. His father, a heavy drinker, refused to work when Jimmy was nine years old. And in a frantic effort to support the family, all of the children who were old enough took whatever jobs they could find. A friend suggested that Jimmy try getting parts in Broadway shows. "From the very beginning," says Lydon, "it was a very ugly experience." He got bit parts in a number of plays before landing featured roles in *Western Waters* (1937), *Sing Out the News* (1938), and *The Happiest Days* (1939). He auditioned, rehearsed, and toured so much that when he was signed for his first movie, *Back Door to Heaven* (1939), he had practically no education and had never seen any kind of a show from the audience.

Freddie Bartholomew[1] was up for the lead in *Tom Brown's School Days* (1940), but Jimmy got it. Freddie played a supporting role. Paramount signed Jimmy in 1941 for a series of B pictures based on the Henry Aldrich[3] character that had proved so popular on stage and radio. Lydon sensed he would be typecast and asked the studio head, Y. Frank Freeman, to put him in other features as well. Freeman's reply: "You're getting paid. Go do your work."

Jimmy starred in nine features of the Aldrich series, beginning with *Henry Aldrich for President* (1941). By the time he completed the last, *Henry Aldrich Plays Cupid* (1944), his screen image was so firmly set he has never been able to shake it. It didn't matter that he had parts in A features—*Life With Father* (1947), *The Time of Your Life* (1948), *The Magnificent Yankee* (1950).

On February 17, 1949, he won the World's Championship for Men's Figure Skating at the Palais de Sports in Paris. *UPI*

DICK BUTTON

The former World Champion figure skater was born on July 18, 1929, in Englewood, New Jersey. When one of Dick's childhood teachers suggested he be given ice-dancing lessons as a remedy for his weight problem, the "fat, little butterball" liked the idea so much he decided right then to be an ice skater. The only childhood Christmas present Dick remembers is a pair of ice skates that went with the decision. Although he tried very hard Dick showed no ability for ice dancing and after failing miserably at Lake Placid in 1942, he made up his mind to become a figure skater.

Six years later, with 191.177 points, Dick won the male figure-skating title at the World Olympics. He repeated his triumph in the 1952 Olympics with 192.256 points. Between his Lake Placid decision and 1952 success, he had taken a second place in the 1943 Eastern States novice competition and the 1944 title in the United States novice competition. He also won the North American, U.S. National, and World titles. His greatest pride is in being the first North American male to win the European men's title. His friend Barbara Ann Scott[2] was the first woman from this continent to take the honor. Although Dick has since been topped in Olympic competition, his point total of 994.7 for compulsory figures and 191.77 for free skating were world records. He is also the first ice skater to do a triple loop, which is still a rarity on ice.

Dick got top billing over Donna Atwood when he skated at some of the playdates during the *Ice Capades of 1952* tour. The show's producer, the late John H. Harris, then married to Donna Atwood, publicized his hand-

Jimmy's chief asset as a juvenile was a very engaging smile and a distinctive voice. But as an adult, he went unnoticed in such pictures as *Island in the Sky* (1953) and *I Passed for White* (1960). Except for those in the audience who remembered him from their Saturday matinee days: "There's Henry Aldrich," they'd say when he came on the screen.

As an adult, his first real professional decision was in 1956 when he decided to work on the other side of the camera. For a year and a half he begged associates in Hollywood to give him a chance. He became a coordinating producer on TV in series such as "McHale's Navy" and "Wagon Train"; then he was associate producer on "77 Sunset Strip" and "Temple Houston" for several seasons. To date he has produced seven features, the best of which is *Chubasco* (1968). In 1972 he worked under Bill Idelson (who used to play Rush on radio's "Vic and Sade") on the "Anna and the King" TV series. Their executive producer was Gene Reynolds, another juvenile actor.

Jimmy is still bitter about the childhood he never had and deeply resents the loss. However, Jimmy was able to send his father money every month until his death a few years ago. But Jimmy's father image (and best friend), from his arrival in Hollywood to this day, is the childless Robert Armstrong (retired and living in Pacific Palisades, California), star of such adventure films as *King Kong*.

The one good thing to come from "Henry Aldrich" was a happy marriage. His mother-in-law was the late Olive Blakeney, who played Mrs. Aldrich. His father-in-law was the late "patent-leather heavy" Bernard Nedell. The Lydons live in the Hollywood Hills with their two daughters. Both want to act. "Not until they are adults," says Jimmy firmly. "I don't like to see any kids on stage or screen. It's unnatural."

Now on the other side of the motion picture camera. *Jerry Goodman*

Donna's farewell tour as Peter Pan in *Ice Capades of 1956.*

DONNA ATWOOD

The star of the Ice Capades was born on Valentine's Day, about 1923, in Newton, Kansas, but moved to Los Angeles as a little girl when her father's health failed. She attended the Mar-Ken School, along with fellow performers the Mauch Twins (Billy is married; Bobby is divorced; both are film editors and live in the San Fernando Valley), Lon McCallister, and the late Virginia Weidler.

Donna was taking dancing lessons at the time she first saw the late Sonja Henie in a movie and decided then that skating was for her. Ice rinks abounded in Los Angeles, and the teen-ager was soon spotted at one by a skating teacher who saw a great potential in her. In 1941, only six months after she had taken up the sport, she took the Junior Ladies' title for the Mercury Figure Skating Club and shared with Eugene Turner the National Pairs championship.

One day in a practice session, the star of the Ice Capades, Belita (Mrs. Jepson Turner of London) noticed Donna on the ice and told her show's producer, the late John H. Harris, about the pretty teen-age girl. Harris and Walter Brown, a major Ice Capades stockholder, and the manager of the Boston Garden, came to the rink to watch Donna practice—technically a violation of nonprofessional rules since it amounted to an audition, which is forbidden to amateurs.

Actually, with the outbreak of the Second World War and the cancellation of national and Olympic meets, there was no reason why she should not turn professional. With her mother's consent, in 1941 she signed a chorus contract with Ice Capades. She never did chorus work.

The Ice Capades toured the United States and Canada most of the year enduring such discomforts of life on the road as cold drab arena-dressing rooms and upper-berth train travel, more suitable to athletes. The Ice Capades was thought of by Harris as a big family and contained an ever-changing pecking order controlled and manipulated by Harris.

some young star as a student skater who would not allow his skating to interfere with his law classes at Harvard. But Dick's large salary, negotiated by his father, was never justified at the Harris box office. He was with the show only ten weeks when he came down with hepatitis. Not long after, Dick starred with *Holiday on Ice* during its Moscow and Leningrad engagements. He also skated on private rinks with Sonja Henie, who wanted him to join her show, but he declined.

Probably the chief reason Button did not pursue a skating career was his yearning to be an actor. Even after receiving his law degree he signed a contract with Twentieth Century-Fox, but no suitable picture was ever found for him. He studied at the Neighborhood Playhouse and appeared in summer stock in such plays as *South Pacific, High Button Shoes,* and *Mister Roberts,* but his acting career never clicked. In 1958 he was seen on the TV special "Hans Brinker and the Silver Skates" with his good friend Tab Hunter. His 1961 Broadway offering *Do You Know the Milky Way?* was a box office disaster and his production of the ice show at the New York World's Fair of 1964 and 1965, with Ronnie Robertson as the star, did disappointing business.

Dick, who is a member of the New York bar, still skates twice a week at the New York Skating Club, but his main interest remains the theatre. He and a partner are preparing to produce a musical in the near future.

Occasionally, Dick narrates skating, water skiing, and gymnastics competition on television for such shows as the "Wide World of Sports." He maintains an office and an apartment in Manhattan and owns property on Staten Island where he is president of the Richmond Town Restoration. He is not married.

The lawyer and producer in his Manhattan office today. *Antoinette Lopopolo*

As the heavy in *The Man They Could Not Hang* (1939).

ROGER PRYOR

The entertainment jack-of-all-trades was born in New York City on August 27, 1901. His father was Arthur Pryor, a band leader who in his time was second in popularity only to John Philip Sousa. Arthur Pryor was adamantly opposed to either of his children pursuing any sort of career in show business.

However, when a New Brunswick, New Jersey, stock company, performing a play called *Adam and Eva*, lost their juvenile lead to illness, eighteen-year-old Roger was offered the part by the producer, a friend of the family. From then on, although his father still frowned on it, Roger toured the country, working in several repertory companies before coming to New York in *The Backslapper* (1925). The play soon closed, but he went right into *The Sea Woman*, which starred Blanche Yurka the same season. He did exceedingly well, working steadily, and in productions that are very well remembered even today. He was with Ruth Gordon in *Saturday's Children* and then went into *The Royal Family*, both in 1927. The next season he replaced Lee Tracy in *The Front Page*.

Roger's biggest personal success was a thinly disguised Walter Winchell in the 1932 hit *Blessed Event*. After seeing Pryor's performance, the only comment from the late columnist, then at the height of his fame and power, was that someone should tell Pryor that he, Winchell, was left-handed.

Even while appearing nightly in his play, his daytime hours went into making his first movie, *Moonlight and Pretzels* (1933), followed by *I Like It That Way* (1934) and *Lady by Choice* (1934). The latter contained the first white telephone in movies, painted by the set designer at the last minute to match Carole Lombard's all-white satin boudoir.

Pryor continued free-lancing in Hollywood right up to *I Live on Danger* (1942) with Jean Parker (divorced and living in Glendale, California).

Harris was also a major stockholder, and he ran the show with an iron hand. Norman Frescott (retired in Studio City, California, with his wife, Benjie, a former Ice-Capet) was the show's manager. Frescott had been a headliner in vaudeville with his mind-reading act, under the billing "The Great Frescott."

To make things even more complicated and difficult for Donna, Harris took a personal interest in her, which served to isolate her from the others. But despite it all, she was well liked by both the staff and performers.

In 1949, Donna married Harris, who was many years her senior, but by then she was the star of the show. Much of the time she was partnered with Bobby Specht (now a manager of one of the Ice Capades shows), a handsome and skilled skater, with an exceptional lack of ego.

Donna starred in the frappé version of "Snow White" in 1949 (taking the 1950 season off to have her twins, Don and Dennis), "The Student Prince" in 1951, "Cinderella" in 1952, "Brigadoon" in 1953, "Snow White" again in 1954, "Wish You Were Here" in 1955, and "Peter Pan" in her farewell tour in 1956. Her favorite was "Peter Pan," and she came out of retirement in 1958 to skate in it for the show's Moscow engagement. This condensed version of the Broadway hit included most of the songs from the original show, plus the patented, invisible Kirby Flying Unit, which was very effective in arenas. Mary Martin, the star of the stage production, in her subsequent TV special also employed the spiral spin.

Not doing so well was the stormy Atwood-Harris marriage, which ended in divorce in 1956, with a large settlement. Donna never remarried. Recently, with her boys off to law school and her daughter Cissy studying drama in New York, Donna sold her big house in West Hollywood and took an apartment overlooking the Pacific Ocean in Marina Del Rey, a private community, where her sons keep their boat. Donna attends Ice Capades openings and parties, where she amazes cast members because of her shyness and genuine surprise when fans and professionals remember her. She spends several afternoons each week at the Ice Capades Chalet in Laurel Canyon, in the San Fernando Valley, giving skating lessons to youngsters who admire her, as she did Sonja Henie.

In her apartment recently at Marina Del Rey, California. *Don Lynn*

She played Miss Watts in the 1939 screen adaption of the hit Broadway play.

RUTH HUSSEY

The leading lady of screen and stage was born Ruth Carol Hussey on October 30, 1914. Her father died when she was seven years old. When Ruth was seventeen her mother remarried, and Ruth took her stepfather's name, O'Rourke, until she began acting in movies. Her surname is pronounced *Huz-ee*.

She studied business and theatre at both Pembroke College and the University of Michigan, playing leads in plays on both campuses before joining the Aimee Loomis Stock Company for a summer. Following that she was a fashion commentator on radio station WPRO in Providence for a year.

When she arrived in New York City, Ruth supported herself as a Powers model before landing the part of Kay, the rich girl, in the touring company of *Dead End*. One night at the end of the second act during the company's Los Angeles engagement, she received a note backstage from Billy Grady, the M-G-M talent scout. Although she hadn't really considered movies, Ruth visited the studio that week, was interviewed, tested, and signed to a contract. She spent the next eight years on the Culver City lot and loved every minute of it.

Her debut in *Madame X* (1937) lasted just long enough for her to murder someone but she quickly graduated to larger parts in *Rich Man, Poor Girl* (1938), with Lew Ayres,[3] *Honolulu* (1939), *The Women* (1939), and *Northwest Passage* (1940). By 1940 she was billed third in the Joan Crawford starrer *Susan and God*. Of her thirty-eight feature films, probably

68

But his efforts were all in programmers such as *Ticket to Paradise* (1936) with Wendy Barrie (living in New York City), *Money and the Woman* (1940), and *She Couldn't Say No* (1941). His one big picture was *Belle of the Nineties* (1934), which had to be made twice. When the first version was sneak-previewed the audience howled, but executives throughout the industry were terrified that its blue humor would bring about enforced government censorship. Its star and author, Mae West, complied, although the second version was far from family fare.

Roger really came into his own on radio in the 1940s. He produced "Cavalcade of America," narrated the NBC Symphony broadcasts, and hosted both "Screen Guild Players" and "Theatre Guild on the Air." His voice was rich, deep, and free of the pretensions so common on network radio of that period. From 1941 to 1945 Roger had his own dance band in which he played trombone. It was one of the better Mickey Mouse bands of its time, and although it provided him with the most personally satisfying period of his career, he was finally driven into bankruptcy with it.

He and the late Kay Francis toured the nation in 1945 in *Windy Hill*, a play by Patsy Ruth Miller[1] produced by the late Ruth Chatterton.

Pryor thereafter directed three quickie features, but refused to allow his name to be used on the credits.

From 1947 until he retired in 1962, Pryor utilized his varied experience as the VP in charge of broadcasting for Foote, Cone & Belding's New York office. (At the time the identical job at Batten, Barton, Durstine & Osborn was held by his late brother.)

Roger confines his activities to fishing and chain smoking these days. He lives with his third wife in an apartment in Pompano Beach, Florida, overlooking the lagoon where his boat is docked. Asked if he missed anything from the past, he replied: "No, and especially not acting. I never felt I was very good and in seventy-two features I don't think I improved very much."

The only one he sees from the old days is his second wife, Ann Sothern.

Completely retired in Florida. *Joan Fiore*

About 1934.

Settled down in one of the antique carriages he collects. *New York Daily News*

JAMES CAGNEY

The little tough guy of the talkies was born on July 17, 1899, of Irish-Norwegian parents in New York City. Jimmy's original plan was to graduate from Columbia University and engage in farming. But he was only in college a short time. He had to leave to help support his family, working at such jobs as a waiter, shipping clerk, and pool-room cue boy. He went into show business for the simple reason that it paid more money than he was making selling newspapers at the time. By 1920 Cagney was dancing in drag in the chorus of *Pitter-Patter,* dressing the star, understudying a principal, and working as a soda jerk at Walgreen's drugstore, all at the same time. His old friend Allen Jenkins, who was in the show with him, remembers Jimmy practically living on coffee and doughnuts during this period so he could give every possible cent he made to his family.

During the run of the play he met and married Frances Willard Vernon, and when he wasn't appearing in such shows as *Outside Looking In* (1925) or *Women Go On Forever* (1927), the couple was touring vaudeville as a dancing team. His first big part was with Joan Blondell in *Maggie the*

her best are *The Philadelphia Story* (1940), for which she was nominated for a supporting Oscar, *H. M. Pulham, Esq.* (1941), *The Uninvited* (1944), and *The Great Gatsby* (1949). Others include *Bedside Manner* (1945), *Louisa* (1950), with Piper Laurie (married and living in Woodstock, New York), *The Lady Wants Mink* (1953), and her last, *The Facts of Life* (1960).

On November 14, 1945, Ruth opened on Broadway as the female lead in the smash hit *State of the Union,* and took over for Madeleine Carroll[2] in *Goodbye, My Fancy* three years later. She also starred in the New York City Center's production of *The Royal Family* in 1951.

During the fifties the actress starred on television on such prestige programs as "Climax," "Lux Video Theatre," and "Studio One." She was nominated for an Emmy for her performance in the title role of *Craig's Wife* in 1954.

If Ruth Hussey had wanted to work more than the little she has during the past fifteen years she certainly could have—her husband, Robert Longenecker, whom she married in 1942, heads his own talent agency. But her painting, golf, horseback riding, and, until recently, her children, have taken up most of her time.

Her oldest son, George, a Navy jet pilot, is a father; her daughter is just finishing college, and her youngest boy, twenty-one, was the recipient of the 1970 Academy Award for the best short, *The Resurrection of Broncho Billy,* which he made as a senior at USC.

Ruth, who lives in a large white formal house in the Brentwood section of Los Angeles, says she enjoyed working with the others in her pictures, but never made great friends. "My real pals were in the make-up department," she says. She has turned down several scripts recently because they were too violent but jumped at the chance to appear last year with old friends Jimmy Stewart and Bob Young on their television shows.

Mary, Ruth, and John, Jr., in their Brentwood, California, home. *Wayne Clark*

Minutes after she was chosen Miss America, September 11, 1948. *UPI*

MISS AMERICA OF 1948

Be Be Shopp was born Beatrice Bella on August 17, 1930, in Berwyn, Illinois, and brought up in nearby Downers Grove. When she was fifteen, her family moved to a farm near Hopkins, Minnesota, where the future Miss America drove a tractor, mixed cement, and cleaned chicken coops.

She first won the title "Miss Hopkins," which didn't impress her greatly. Hopkins was so small there was hardly any competition. In fact, she had to be urged to enter the Miss Minnesota finals. And winning that one automatically put her in the running for the big one in Atlantic City.

She had just turned eighteen, the youngest and the busiest of the entries (only Miss America of 1954 has equaled her 37"). Although pleased to be one of the forty-eight contestants, Be Be wasn't at all nervous; she was sure that her age and lack of sophistication would rule her out of serious consideration. But she won the judges over, playing "Claire de Lune" on her vibraharp. She was pronounced the winner, with Miss Wyoming placing second, and Miss Kansas (Vera Ralston, who later became a movie star under the name Vera Miles) third.

In the vernacular of her hometown, she was a big, strapping farm girl—5 feet 9 inches. But with her brown hair, blue-green eyes, and baby face, Be Be proved to be far more controversial than her appearance would indicate.

She was the first Miss America to visit Europe during her reign, and the foreign press had a field day asking her about her baby fat, sex, and alcohol. Be Be's moral judgments remain strictly Middle America but she is not the prude reporters tried to make her out. They quoted her as strongly disapproving of bikinis (at the time worn mostly by the most daring) and

Magnificent (1929). The following year the two were costarred in *Penny Arcade* and both signed a contract with Warner Brothers from that show.

Jimmy's first feature film was *Sinners' Holiday* (1930) but it was in *Public Enemy* (1931) that he hit big. He was playing the second lead in this film, but after a few days of shooting the director and producer agreed that Jimmy should swap roles with Eddie Woods. Although the picture made him a star overnight, that role and the many others like it forged an image Cagney grew to resent. Though he acted the good guy in many features, the public always seemed to remember him as the tough guy. Audiences felt that nobody was better than Jimmy when he was bad. Whether the part called for him to brutalize a woman, machine-gun a speakeasy, cover a headline story, arrest a gangster, or mastermind a jail break, Cagney came across with absolute authority and seemed particularly to relish the dirty work.

Such films as *Mayor of Hell* (1933), *G-Men* (1935), *Angels With Dirty Faces* (1938), and *The Fighting 69th* (1940) were box-office winners at the time of their release and gained him a whole new generation of fans when they played on television years later.

After leaving Warner's in 1940 he free-lanced, making such pictures as *Blood on the Sun* (1945), *The Time of Your Life* (1948), which was a box-office failure he made with his own company, *A Lion in the Streets* (1953), and *Mister Roberts* (1955). Playing Moe "the Gimp" Snyder (heads Chicago's City Hall mailroom) in *Love Me or Leave Me* (1955), he was again nominated for an Oscar (he won an Oscar for *Yankee Doodle Dandy* in 1942). Cagney directed *Short Cut to Hell* (1957) and co-produced and starred in *The Gallant Hours* (1960). His last film appearance was in *One, Two, Three* (1961), although he narrated *Arizona Bushwackers* (1968).

Cagney always maintained that he was in acting only for the money, which seems hard to believe since he was named one of the top ten box-office draws in the world for six of his starring years. His many quarrels with Warner's and suspensions were always over money rather than roles. The feisty actor was considered a problem by the front office, although his conduct on the set was strictly professional, and he is still one of the most respected and best liked stars of that period among his peers.

The star who in 1941 was the second highest paid citizen in the United States (Louis B. Mayer was first) is now doing the farming he always longed for on his estates on Martha's Vineyard and in Stanfordville, New York, where he is the neighbor of his longtime friend Robert Montgomery.[3] His two adopted children, a boy and girl, are now grown and the Cagneys are grandparents. As a gentleman farmer Jimmy has time to paint and even has a tutor to help him along. When he announced his retirement many of his colleagues were skeptical but he has refused even to appear on any TV talk show or allow photos to be taken. He turned down the plum part of Doolittle in the 1964 film version of *My Fair Lady* and nixed the offer to play Judge Julius Hoffman in the proposed film about the Chicago Seven conspiracy trial involving Abbie Hoffman and the others over the 1968 Democratic Convention riots. True to his movie image, Cagney meant what he said.

Six years at M-G-M in the forties.

TOM DRAKE

The nice young man from 1940s movies was born Alfred Alderdeiss in the Flatbush section of Brooklyn on August 5, 1919, and was brought up in New Rochelle, New York. By 1937, his parents had died, and he and his sister moved to Manhattan so he could pursue an acting career.

In 1938 he debuted in *June Night,* which closed during its Philadelphia tryout. The following year he did *Clean Beds* on Broadway. M-G-M caught his performance opposite Joan Caulfield (living in Los Angeles) and signed him to a contract—after changing his name to Tom Drake.

It was not the best time for a young man to be under contract to a major studio. These were war years and most of the pictures being made centered on young women. And if there was a plum part suitable for Tom, it usually went to Van Johnson. Although he liked Louis B. Mayer personally, he objected to some of the pictures he was cast in. "But I made the mistake of doing them anyway," he confided. "I should have held my ground like Monty Clift. They would have had more respect for me." It was Montgomery Clift who got the part in the screen version of *The Glass Menagerie,* which Tom wanted badly. Two other disappointments were *The Sea of Grass* and *Strangers on a Train,* with roles that went to Robert Walker.

Tom's first picture was *The White Cliffs of Dover* (1944), but his part was edited out before it was released. However, his work in it was so good that Arthur Freed tapped him for the delightful *Meet Me in St. Louis* (1944). But the film he is probably best remembered for is *The Green Years* (1946). Ironically, the producer didn't think Tom was right for the movie and only through trickery did Tom manage to test and win the role.

falsies—a hotly debated subject in postwar America. She had never said anything about either, except that she never wore them. The U.S. press picked up from the Continent stories that misquoted her and that invented her behavior. "Miss America's Moral Crusade" was how the Europeans reported it. Her father, who was the head of the health and education department of the company that owned Cream of Wheat, claimed it was the Communists who were making those things up about his daughter. When a story that had her frequenting bars was published, he phoned her chaperone to check it out.

The *New York Daily News* came to Be Be's rescue with a lenghty editorial entitled, "Thanks, Miss America," denouncing the foreign press and hailing Be Be for being so outspoken.

After her reign, in 1949, Be Be entered the Manhattan School of Music on a scholarship, and then toured the country with two young men as the Be Be Shopp Trio. In 1953 she hosted a women's show on a local Minneapolis TV station.

Full retirement came in 1954 when she married Bayard Waring, one of the only two men she dated who made her feel they wanted to take her out, not Miss America.

If there were to be a title of Mrs. America, Be Be would probably win it even though she has four teen-age daughters. She is active in civic affairs, and helps her husband run their restaurant, The Spinning Wheel, in Redding, Connecticut. "It's not fancy or gourmet but it sure is good," says Be Be. They live nearby in Weston, where her crown rests on the mantle of their large New England style house. Mrs. Waring, who has been back to the Miss America pageant eighteen times, and once in 1953 served as a judge, thinks it needs much updating.

Had she any regrets? "Heavens no! My whole life has been very happy."

With author Frank Deford ("There She Is") recently. *Michael Knowles*

In the mid-1940s, undisputedly the "Queen of the B's" on the Twentieth Century-Fox lot.

LYNN BARI

The star of early TV and the "other woman" of feature films was born Marjorie Schuyler Fisher on December 18, 1919, in Roanoke, Virginia. When she was seven years old, her stepfather, a Religious Science minister, was transferred to Boston where she attended very good private schools. The family came to Hollywood when she was 12.

Answering a newspaper ad for tall chorus girls, Lynn landed an $8.43-a-day job dancing in the Joan Crawford starrer *Dancing Lady* (1933). She remembers swooning over the costar Clark Gable, who used to call her "jail bait." The picture's choreographer, Sammy Lee, got her a stock contract at Twentieth Century-Fox. There she labored in such B pictures as *Spring Tonic* (1935), *Lancer Spy* (1937), and *Charter Pilot* (1940), until she did *Blood and Sand* (1941); its star, Tyrone Power, was one of her great crushes. Lynn also had a good part in the A feature *The Magnificent Jerk* (1942), but was again returned to the back lot for low-budget features; she was often a woman with a gun in her purse. Not surprisingly, she loathes guns. The only time she caused a delay on a set was when she had to fire one. She would close her eyes tight. "I made as many [pictures] as three at a time," says Lynn. "I'd go from one set to another shooting people and stealing husbands." Of the pace, she says it was "so fast I never knew what the hell the plots were." She was disappointed in the quality of *The Bridge of San Luis Rey* (1944), which had a rushed production schedule. Her studio requested a unique fee for loaning her to appear with the late Akim Tamiroff and Joan Loring (married to a doctor and living in Manhattan): a piece of equipment, still referred to on the Fox lot as "the Bari boom." Some of her other movies were *Margie* (1946), *The Kid from Cleveland* (1949), and *Francis Joins the Wacs* (1954). She was a great favorite at Fox

Though he dated Judy Garland, Gloria DeHaven, and Cardinal Spellman's niece, Tom didn't get the space in fan magazines some of the young actors with flashier looks rated. However, he is remembered for being a much better actor than the glamour boys of the era.

He did not enjoy working with a collie in *The Courage of Lassie* (1946), and the failure of *The Beginning of the End* (1947) was a disappointment to him. He played Richard Rodgers in *Words and Music* (1948) and was in *Mr. Belvedere Goes to College* (1949) with Alan Young (a Christian Science lecturer who lives in Laguna Beach, California).

Not much went well for him after he left M-G-M in 1950. He was seen in B films such as *Sangaree* (1953) and *Johnny Reno* (1966). In the western *Warlock* (1959), he was billed fifth, and the lavish *Raintree County* (1957) was a box-office disaster. In *The Sandpiper* (1965) his part was small.

Tom did a few European pictures during a residency of several years in Rome, but he has found the going rather rough since his return to Hollywood. He says that young casting directors either don't remember him or he's considered "merchandise that's been around too long to get excited about." He recently made an unreleased low-budget picture, and occasionally gets a guest shot on a TV show, such as "Marcus Welby, M.D."

Many fans and critics thought Tom seldom had a chance to prove what a sensitive, honest actor he was, and Tom is determined to make it again in the new Hollywood. He not only has licked a serious drinking problem but quit smoking, as well. Both habits may have contributed to his changed, deep, authoritative voice that he feels will eventually get used as a cop or a heavy—hopefully also in a running part on a TV series.

In the meantime, the perennial bachelor supports himself mainly by selling used cars practically across the street from the Metro lot, in Culver City.

Today he would like to play policemen or heavies.

In *The Yearling*, which earned him an Oscar.

CLAUDE JARMAN, JR.

The boy who won an Oscar for his first movie role was born on September 14, 1934, in Nashville, Tennessee.

One day when Claude was ten years old a man who was supposed to be a building inspector spent a few minutes observing his class. After school he was called to the principal's office where the man told him that he would drop by his house that evening to speak with his parents. When the man arrived he found that the boy was out and had neglected to mention the incident to his mother and father. He was at a Cub Scout meeting. The man introduced himself to the Jarmans as Clarence Brown, the director of such movies as *Anna Christie* and *The Human Comedy*. He had picked Claude, who was badly in need of a haircut at the time, as a candidate to star in the screen adaptation of the Marjorie Kinnan Rawlings best seller, *The Yearling*. Disappointed in not being able to interview the boy further, and photograph him, Brown left.

Mr. Jarman, a railroad employee, and his wife were quite disappointed, as the director explained that since he had to leave that night it was unlikely that he would be able to see Claude. That evening a snowstorm, rare in Nashville, grounded all planes. Brown returned, talked with Claude, took a photo of him, and promised the Jarmans they would hear from him, one way or the other, within a month.

Three weeks later, Claude, who had acted in a few school plays but had no theatrical ambitions and had never even heard of *The Yearling*, was on his way to M-G-M, where he remained under contract for five years.

during her fourteen years under contract, thanks to her unpretentious, direct manner.

Entering TV early, Lynn starred on the live series "The Detective's Wife" on CBS in 1950 and followed it with "Boss Lady," a widely syndicated series.

Her marriages earned her as much newspaper space as her film roles. In 1943 she divorced her first husband, Walter Kane, after five years. Asked what his job with Howard Hughes was all about, the former Mrs. Kane referred to him as a sort of talent scout. Next, she wed Sid Luft prior to his marriage to Judy Garland. The five-year union produced a son, a great deal of publicity over his custody during the divorce proceedings, and much bitterness. She now recalls that the experience had cost her $1 million. Finally, a divorce from Beverly Hills psychiatrist Dr. Nathan Rickles in 1972 was without fanfare. But Lynn had no qualms in divulging in an interview highly personal details of her seventeen years with him. She got a $150,000 settlement and a letter from him stating she is free to write a book about their goings-on in their home (her husband analyzed some of Hollywood's top stars there).

Lynn's fans recognized a quality in her work that is very evident on the stage but that never really was developed in films. On her 111-city tour with *Barefoot in the Park* in 1965 and again with *The Gingerbread Lady* in 1972 she got star billing and excellent notices.

And as in the days of Fox, she is popular with her associates. The young players on her tours like her frankness and salty language. Always well groomed and smartly dressed, Lynn lives alone in a very pretty apartment just off the Sunset Strip. The staunch liberal voted for Dr. Spock in the 1972 presidential election.

Mary and Dana Andrews congratulate their old friend on her opening night in *The Gingerbread Lady*.

In 1928, Jack's career and investments were doing very well.

JACK MULHALL

The durable leading man of the screen was born John Joseph Francis Mulhall on October 7, 1887, in Wappingers Falls, New York. As a boy he sang Irish songs with a traveling show, acted in a stock company, and toured vaudeville with Ned Wayburn.

While studying art in New York City, Rex Ingram, the motion-picture pioneer director, got him a job at $5 a day acting in films made in the Bronx by Thomas Edison's company. Jack made a number of one-reelers, including one that had sound throughout. He was also active at the Biograph Studios, in Manhattan, where he appeared in *Hard Cash* (1913) and *House of Discord* (1913). Biograph brought him to Los Angeles on New Year's Day, 1914, with the promise of a $15-a-week salary plus $14 in expense money. He was seen in such features as *Tides of Retribution* (1915) and *Madame Spy* (1917).

Mulhall lasted much longer than nearly all his contemporaries, but never achieved a status where he could carry a picture by himself. He had a breezy Irish affability that was agreeable to audiences and it served him well in getting along with his leading ladies. During his heyday he played opposite screen immortals such as Mabel Normand in *Mickey* (1918), Marguerite Clark in *All of a Sudden Peggy* (1920), Alice Terry (living in North Hollywood, California) in *Turn to the Right* (1927), Constance Talmadge[1] in *Dulcy* (1923), Norma Talmadge in *The Girl From Coney Island* (1926), and Colleen Moore[3] in *Orchids and Ermine* (1927). He had contracts with Universal, Metro, and Joseph Schenck before signing with First

Brown, who earlier had brought Butch Jenkins[3] and Liz Taylor to prominence, coaxed a smooth, natural performance out of Claude—which in 1946 brought Claude a special, miniature Academy Award for his portrayal of the boy who loved a baby deer.

Claude's second film was *High Barbaree* (1947), and then came *Intruder in the Dust* (1949), a Faulkner story, which was a critical success but too far ahead of its time to win much favor with the public.

Claude never enjoyed making films—at least not the acting end of it. "I didn't hate it," he now says, "but neither did I find it at all fulfilling." Before his last, *The Great Locomotive Chase* (1956), he appeared in *The Sun Comes Up* (1949), *Hangman's Knot* (1952), with Randolph Scott,[3] and *Fair Wind to Java* (1953).

During his layoff periods at the studio he would return to Tennessee, where he worked in an ice cream factory. After M-G-M he went home again to attend Vanderbilt University, thereafter joining the Navy. In 1959, he got a discharge, he got married, and he appeared on a segment of TV's "Wagon Train." He was divorced in 1967, and in 1968 married his second wife, Mary Ann.

From 1960 to 1968 he was the West Coast public relations director for John Hancock Insurance. He is now president of Medion Productions, which produced the rock feature *Fillmore* (1972), and executive director of the San Francisco Film Festival. He lives with his wife and five children on a ranch in Napa, California.

On the wall of his San Francisco office hangs his photo taken that night long ago in Nashville by Clarence Brown (retired and living in Palm Springs), whom he still sees regularly. Although Claude very much enjoys the production side of the movie business, he has no interest in acting again, and would not permit any of his children to perform until they were out of school and capable of making that decision themselves.

In front of his office in downtown San Francisco. *Lauren Eason*

Radio's Portia from the early forties. *NBC*

"PORTIA FACES LIFE"

At 5:15 P.M. EST on October 7, 1940, the preamble "Portia Faces Life . . . a story reflecting the courage, spirit, and integrity of American women everywhere" was heard for the first time, over NBC stations from coast to coast. In its opening episode, the soap's heroine, Portia Blake, who also happened to be a lawyer, wife, and mother, learned that her husband had just been killed. Although the series continued for nearly twelve years with five fiftcen-minute programs a week (each rehearsed one hour), only few of the thousands of episodes that followed were less traumatic.

Writer Mona Kent created the character who was modeled and first named after Shakespeare's heroine in *The Merchant of Venice*. Mona and the show's sponsor, General Foods, chose Chicago-born Lucille Wall for the title role, in which she remained up to the last broadcast. For the first seven years *Portia* was on the air, Lucille did not have a vacation because the musicians' union would not allow the network to record the show's theme, "Kerry Dance," and listeners had become so used to her voice that the producers did not want to chance using another woman.

For many years Lucille concurrently acted the part of Belle on the "Lorenzo Jones" soap, which was carried by the same network at 4:30 P.M. A great tribute to Miss Wall's acting skills is the fact that very few listeners realized that Belle Jones, a very simple, highly domesticated housewife, was the same person who forty-five minutes later became the valiant, sophisticated woman attorney.

Although she competed in a man's world as a criminal lawyer, neither Portia nor her listeners ever forgot she was a woman. Portia eventually married Walter Manning who was to be a father for her son Dickie and a

National where he and Dorothy Mackaill costarred in a series that enjoyed great popularity in the twenties. *Joanna* (1925) and *Lady Be Good* (1928) were among the dozen they made. But when Dorothy's contract expired and she wouldn't renew, the studio dropped Mulhall.

Jack's voice was fine for the arrival of talkies; his last with Mackail, *Two Weeks Off* (1929), was partly sound, and in *Dark Streets* (1929) he played a dual role, a first in sound films. But his kind of parts were being taken over by younger actors, such as James Dunn and Robert Montgomery. Jack worked frantically in the early thirties in such features as *Show Girl in Hollywood* (1930), with Alice White (working in an office in Hollywood), and *Lover Come Back* (1931). It was a desperate attempt to recoup some of the losses he suffered in the Great Crash. In 1930 alone he appeared in eight features, but he wasn't able to land another studio contract paying him his usual $3,500 a week, nor could he any longer command $5,000 for free-lance services. Between *Mystery Squadron* (1933) and *Dick Tracy vs. Crime* (1941), with the late Ralph Byrd, he made eight serials. It didn't help much because in 1935, with $6,000 in assets and liabilities over $350,000, he declared bankruptcy. There were a few mediocre features like *Beloved Enemy* (1936), with Brian Aherne (living in Vevey, Switzerland) and *The Storm* (1938), with the late Barton MacLane, but by the forties he was reduced to walk-ons and bit parts, some even without dialogue. Old friends helped him get small parts on TV dramas in the fifties, but he supported himself mainly as the greeter at a Hollywood restaurant.

Today the man who had appeared in over a thousand motion pictures lives modestly with his wife of fifty years in the same apartment building as Nick Lucas, just off Hollywood Boulevard. He lunches almost every day with old cronies at the Masquers Club.

Beside his tree last Christmas. *Robert G. Youngson*

With the author at WBAI-FM studios in New York. *Michael Knowles*

The burlesque queen in 1942.

GEORGIA SOTHERN

The highly popular burlesque queen was born Hazel Anderson, in Dunganon, Georgia, about 1917. Shortly after, her father abandoned her and her mother. Mrs. Anderson eked out a living for them selling short stories to women's magazines, writing under the name Corey Estelle.

By the time Georgia was four years old she and her mother were living in Atlanta, where her uncle was an actor with the local stock company. One day when a little girl in one of the plays got sick, the uncle suggested she be replaced by Georgia. Georgia did so well, and liked it so much, that for the next nine years mother and daughter toured the vaudeville circuits, with Georgia working in a variety of acts as an acrobat, toe dancer, singer, and actress.

In 1931, with vaudeville on its last legs, Georgia was stranded in Philadelphia when her show folded. When she heard a man was hiring young girls at the Bijou Theatre, she went for an audition. She learned it was a burlesque house and that the opening was for a stripper. All she knew of burlesque was that it embarrassed her mother whenever the subject came lean-on for Portia. She would have been better off fending for herself because Walter seemed to be the source of most of their difficulty in their home on Peach Street.

Dickie was played by a number of young actors, among them Skippy Homeier. Another boy who played Dickie was Ivan Cury (now a staff director at CBS-TV in New York City). The year before the show went off the air, the Mannings had a daughter, Sheilah. But "Portia Faces Life" ended on a sour note. After a dramatic trial, Portia Manning, the attorney who had saved the lives and fortunes of so many in the courtroom, was herself sentenced to prison on charges the audience knew were false; the writers, who had hoped for a public outcry that would force the network to bring the series back, had framed her.

In 1954 CBS Television revived the series, with Fran Carlon as Portia. Walter on this short-lived program was played by Karl Swenson, who had played Lorenzo Jones with Lucille. She still sees Swenson, who is active in Hollywood as an actor and director.

Lucille was as close to a star as radio ever produced. She got a large salary, top billing, and lived quite fittingly on Manhattan's chic Sutton Place. For over a decade now she has been living in Los Angeles. She rises at 5 A.M. several mornings a week for her running part as Nurse March on ABC Television's daytime soap opera, "General Hospital." A widow in real life, Lucille plays a spinster nurse who has just married an outpatient at the hospital. Her new husband, defined as a bachelor before his marriage, is played by 1930s movie star Tom Brown.

To this day, nearly every fan letter she receives, though addressed to the "General Hospital" soap, mentions her roles as Portia and Belle. Asked whatever became of Portia, Lucille says: "The housewives' Perry Mason is as far as I know still in the clink!"

Lucille in her dressing room at ABC-TV in Hollywood. *Beth Anne Phillips*

A typical Blue pose in 1937 for Paramount.

BEN BLUE

The dancer-comedian was born in Montreal in 1902 and raised in Baltimore by his father, D. A. Bernstein, an art and antique dealer. Ben's parents were divorced when he was very young. At thirteen he came to New York where he was for a time a haberdashery salesman and window dresser at Macy's. Then he got a job imitating Chaplin on the street in front of a nickelodeon. His pantomime was so good someone sent him to try out for the chorus of a Broadway show. Although Ben never studied dancing and claims he has no ear for music, he had been dancing on his own since he was nine years old. He went into the chorus of *Irene* (1919) and eventually became an understudy. He also did chorus work in *Mary* (1920).

By the time he was twenty years old Ben Blue had opened a chain of dancing schools in the Midwest, partnered with Tony De Marco. Then he went to Los Angeles, where he began working with Milt Britton's Band and on the vaudeville circuits. It was during that time that he developed his most famous routine, Death of a Swan, which he performs in a tutu. That skit was a particular favorite with audiences in London where he spent three years during the twenties.

Before sound came to motion pictures Blue made comedy shorts for both Warner Brothers and Hal Roach. When talkies arrived he began making feature films and had contracts with M-G-M and Paramount. By his own count he has appeared in nearly two hundred movies. A few are *High, Wide and Handsome* (1937), *Cocoanut Grove* (1938), and *Paris Honeymoon* (1939), with Franceska Gaal (the late Mrs. Francis de Dajkovich of Manhattan). After time out in 1940 to marry Axie Dunlap, a showgirl he met

up. Accepting the job might upset her mother and so when asked her name she told the theatre manager, who had already commented on her Southern drawl, "Georgia Sothern." She planned to work only a few weeks for the tempting $50 weekly salary, before returning to vaudeville.

Georgia's recollection of her debut on the runway: "I didn't know a damn thing about what I was supposed to do other than dance and take my clothes off. I still don't know what I did out there but it brought the house down. I was quite mature for thirteen and they liked me. Well, I liked them right back. The stripping part never bothered me for a minute. And my mother was so happy about the $50 she wasn't even embarrassed."

Within two months, she was signed by the Minskys to headline at their Republic Theatre on 42nd Street. She stayed with them fifteen years, earning up to $3,500 a week. During the thirties and forties when she wasn't at Minsky's, Georgia got top billing at virtually every major burlesque house in the country. Fellow strippers Gypsy Rose Lee and Peaches Strange (both deceased) were her closest friends.

Georgia occasionally appeared on her own at the height of her career, playing state fairs that paid her up to $5,000 a day, thanks to her shrewdly insisting on a percentage of the take. Mike Todd featured her on Broadway in his shows *Star and Garter* (1942) and *The Naked Genius* (1943), thereafter hitting the road with the Ritz Brothers (very active on TV) in a tour of presentation houses.

Increasingly, Georgia appeared in summer stock from the late forties through the fifties, acting in such plays as *Personal Appearance* and *Burlesque*. She stripped, but only for the top houses, who could pay her salary, and they became rare. In 1955 she married attorney John J. Diamond, and they and their poodle now live in the same Manhattan apartment house as silent screen star Aileen Pringle.[2]

Star strippers in Georgia's day prided themselves on being distinctive. Georgia's billing was "Perpetual Motion" and "Dynamite" (only a slight overstatement). She opened her act with "Georgia on my Mind." "Tiger Rag" ("Hold that tiger . . .") closed it. Georgia was fast and energetic and it accounted for her fame. When Georgia worked, the boys got their money's worth.

The ex-stripper who loved burlesque and the people in it says: "It quit me. I would never have left the business if it hadn't changed so much. It got so nobody cared. I worked as late as 1968 at the 46th Street Theatre in New York City, but it was dead. The audience, the strippers—the whole business."

Today Georgia has great hopes of doing a Broadway show based on one she did at the Lambs' club, called *Melba, the Toast of Pithole.* Her autobiography, which is called *Georgia,* edited by her close friend Mickey Spillane, has recently been published—in paperback. "They wanted me to make it dirtier," she says, "but my life just wasn't that dirty. Errol Flynn and I were crazy about each other but I never went to bed with him. I was dying to but wouldn't give him the satisfaction. Should I fib and make him out to be an even bigger lover or tell the truth and let a lot of people down? I'm still deciding."

when they were both appearing in *George White's Scandals* in 1939, Ben made *Panama Hattie* (1942), *Broadway Rhythm* (1944), and *Easy to Wed* (1946). His last feature was the all-star comedy *It's a Mad, Mad, Mad, Mad World* (1963).

Because he is a visual performer the only medium in which Ben did not succeed is radio, but he enjoyed a long and profitable run in television on the "Colgate Comedy Hour" and "Saturday Nite Revue" during the fifties.

Ben Blue owned and operated "Slapsie" Maxie's nightclubs in both Los Angeles and San Francisco for a number of years and had a club under his own name in Santa Monica, which he closed in 1961 after six years. Jackie Gleason's engagement at Blue's club was a major stepping-stone in the comic's career.

Axie Blue is now a professional artist, as is their son. Ben also paints, and he owned an art gallery in West Hollywood in 1971, which lasted two weeks. But he spends most of his time playing golf, "very poorly," he admits. His hilltop house is filled with canvases and sculptures done by himself and his family, as well as those he has collected. The general quality of the art was summed up by a local dealer: "Vincent Price would buy up the whole lot and retail it at Sears, Roebuck."

Ben dislikes talking about his career or show business but when he does talk he is almost contemptuous. The only reason he would ever work again is to alleviate boredom, and his only goal as a performer was to earn enough to quit. He has kept no clippings about himself, and his modern Beverly Hills home lacks even a single photograph. On a recent radio program he disclosed he has no friends in show business since he never socialized with show people. "They don't interest me at all. You can live in my house for fifty years and never hear show business mentioned."

The art collector in his Beverly Hills home. *Alicia Rosinek*

She played Mama on television from 1949 to 1957.

PEGGY WOOD

The star of Broadway and television was born in Brooklyn February 9, 1892. Her father was a well-known humorist and newspaperman of the era. After Peggy hummed the Wedding March from *Lohengrin,* at the age of four, both parents encouraged her to sing. By eight, she was taking formal lessons. One of her coaches was the eminent Emma Calvé.

Peggy was in the chorus of the 1910 Broadway production of *Naughty Marietta.* Seven years and seven featured roles later, she was the toast of the Great White Way in Victor Herbert's *Maytime,* which she also took on tour.

Peggy Wood's career in the theatre could be envied by almost any stage actress. She was versatile enough to sing and dance in musicals, such as *Buddies* (1919) and *Bitter Sweet,* in which she made her London debut in 1929 at the behest of Noel Coward, and in *The Cat and the Fiddle* (1932). Yet she was taken seriously enough as an actress to have been asked by the legendary John Drew to play opposite him in the national tour of *Trelawny of the "Wells"* (1927). And George Arliss had her as his Portia in *The Merchant of Venice* (1928) on Broadway and on the road. Two of the greatest successes of her career were the comedies *Candida* (1925) and *Blithe Spirit* (1941). Some of her other Broadway appearances were in *Miss Quis* (1937), *The Happiest Years* (1949), and *The Girls in 509* (1958). One of her favorite roles was the bitchy novelist opposite Jane Cowl in *Old Acquaintance* (1940). Through it all Peggy never got a really bad personal notice.

For all her acclaim on stage, where she was a favorite of audiences as well as fellow actors for her kindness and professionalism, she was almost completely wasted in movies. And there was also the personal treatment. When Irving Thalberg at M-G-M learned that she was one of the founders of

Actors Equity, he had her outgoing mail opened for fear she was giving any aid to the Screen Actors Guild then forming. About her films, Peggy says: "I wasn't pretty in the way one was supposed to be out there and I think they just gave up on me. They didn't know where to put me and the fact that I could act confused them terribly." She did make a number of films: *Jalna* (1931), *A Star Is Born* (1937), and *Dream Girl* (1948). In her part as the Abbess in *The Sound of Music* (1965), she was so covered with a nun's habit that few recognized her.

It was the TV series "Mama," which was adapted from the best seller and Broadway hit *I Remember Mama,* that made Peggy a national star. When it premiered on CBS on July 1, 1949, one network executive gave it thirteen weeks at the most. It lasted until June 1, 1957, and continued for years in reruns. Peggy brought to the part of Mama Hanson all her experience as an actress, wife, and mother. One of her many awards was the Royal St. Olaf medal presented to her in Norway by King Haakon. She is still stopped often in public by fans. Many are in their late twenties and grew up watching the tales of the Norwegian immigrant family making their way in pre-WWI America. Her characterization had warmth and depth and the series is considered a high mark in TV family drama. She still occasionally sees members of the cast Judson Laire (living in New York City and active on TV), Dick Van Patten (living in Los Angeles and also acting), and Rosemary Rice (married and living in Chicago). Robin Morgan, who played little Dagmar, is married and is an active and militant feminist in New York City.

Peggy has a house in Stamford, Connecticut, and an apartment on Park Avenue. Since 1941, she has been the wife of businessman William H. Walling. Her first husband, John V. A. Weaver, a playwright and poet, died in 1938. She has a son and three grandchildren. Although poor health has discouraged her from acting for some years, she is a frequent theatregoer, both on- and off-Broadway.

Outside her Manhattan apartment house recently. *Ellis St. Joseph*

With wife, Valerie Hobson, in 1961 just before he met Christine Keeler. *UPI*

JOHN PROFUMO

The Englishman whose affair with a call girl brought down the Macmillan government was born on January 30, 1915, into a wealthy family of Italian descent. In 1940, he became the youngest member of Parliament, but lost his seat in the Labour landslide of 1945. After serving with his country's mission in Japan, he was returned to the House of Commons in 1950. He then began his rapid rise in the Tory party from Joint Parliamentary Secretary in 1952 to Minister of State for Foreign Affairs in 1959. In July of 1960 he became Secretary of State for War and a member of the Prime Minister's Cabinet.

Just before the scandal broke, he was described in an English book on the landed gentry: "He lives in fashionable Chester Terrace and leads a well-modulated life of diligent work and moderate play (hunting and cinematography). His wife is the former film star Valerie Hobson. He entertains politicos, industrialists and foreign visitors in quiet, excellent style."

Profumo met Christine Keeler[3] in July of 1961 through Dr. Stephen Ward, an osteopath by profession and a procurer by inclination. Through Miss Keeler, he became friends with her sometime lover, Eugene "Honey Bear" Ivanov, a member of the Soviet Embassy. Ivanov encouraged Christine's affair with Profumo and persuaded her to try to find out when certain atomic secrets were to be given to West Germany. And Ivanov personally attempted to get Profumo to persuade his government to intervene during the Cuban missile crisis.

In August of 1961, a British security officer warned Profumo of his relationship and took the matter to higher-ups in the government. But they refused to believe the story. Newspapers had heard of the goings-on long before the story broke, but they were afraid to publish anything because of Britain's stringent libel laws. In February of 1963, the Tory Whip confronted Profumo with a note Profumo had written Christine. It began, "Darling," but Profumo explained it to his colleague's satisfaction. (Because of his smoothness of manner, Profumo's nickname had long been "the head waiter.")

On March 21, Labour members began asking embarrassing questions on the floor of Parliament. Two days later, with the Prime Minister at his side, Profumo stood up in the House of Commons and not only categorically denied that he had ever known Miss Keeler sexually, but threatened a libel suit against anyone who made further allegations. That done, he went straight to the races with his good friend the Queen Mother and that evening attended a ball as her guest.

Two days later, he was accused over the BBC of being a security risk. And what had been rumors until then became outright accusations. Profumo was summoned back from his vacation in Italy, and on June 4, 1963, was confronted with testimony from Ward and Keeler. It contradicted everything he had sworn to. Admitting that he had lied, he tendered his resignation.

Harold Macmillan had been made to look like a fool and his party was swept out of office the following year. The nobleman, elected official, graduate of Harrow and Oxford, with the training, background, and right to rule, had let his family, party, and country down. For all his manners and privileges Profumo was without honor. The case unleashed long-dormant resentment of the Establishment that has yet to subside.

Profumo and his wife and son were never arrested, harassed, or caused any financial hardship. Since 1964, he has commuted from his Hertfordshire home to Toynbee Hall, a grimy red-brick settlement house in the London slums. There, legal and medical services are provided for the destitute. During a recent visit to the hall by Elizabeth II, she was photographed smiling her approval of his accomplishments, thus conferring on Profumo a new respectability. But the Profumos had remained socially quite acceptable, quietly if not publicly, by their highly placed friends, some of whom no doubt were grateful that they were not implicated in a case far more involved than it appeared.

The Queen's smile has brought Profumo back from obscurity and disgrace. *Popperfoto*

Vivian Smolen emoting during one of "Our Gal Sunday"'s last broadcasts in 1956. *CBS Radio*

"OUR GAL SUNDAY"

The durable soap opera that unfolded the trials and tribulations of "an orphan girl named Sunday from the little mining town of Silver Creek, Colorado, who in young womanhood married England's richest, most handsome lord, Lord Henry Brinthrope" all began on CBS Radio in March 29, 1937, and was based on the Broadway play *Sunday,* in which Ethel Barrymore in 1904 delivered the now-famous line: "That's all there is. There isn't any more."

"Sunday" was produced by radio's most successful team, Frank and Anne Hummert (widow Anne lives in Manhattan), and was heard for most of its run at 12:45 P.M. EST, just following "The Romance of Helen Trent."[3] The setting was Lord Brinthrope's huge estate, Black Swan Hall, somewhere in Virginia. The plots of the various episodes, which were nearly always absurd, usually found Sunday being put upon by her in-laws who felt that Lord Henry had married beneath his station.

Vivian Smolen, who auditioned for and took over the role from originator Dorothy Lowell in 1946, played it as directed—sweet, understanding, and long suffering. She was so saccharine sweet that many listeners compared her to Melanie in the film *Gone With the Wind.* Part of the reason was the similarity of Melanie's husband's accent to the English accent of Sunday's husband, played originally by Karl Swenson (living in Los Angeles) and then replaced by Alistair Duncan (residing in Sydney, Australia). Leslie Howard had played Melanie's husband, Ashley, in *Gone With the Wind,* and the radio producers played upon the similarity, although Lord Henry was much less noble. The constant put-downs Sunday endured from the class-conscious snobs around her helped confirm the anti-English feelings that were common in Mid-America.

Sunday tried always to lead a quiet, simple life even though she was supposed to be very rich and live in a castle. Her life, however, was constantly in a state of turmoil. What she did most and best was to stand by Henry while he risked financial ruin or carried on with another woman or was kidnapped or had insomnia or even when he disappeared and his identical twin took his place. In the twin episodes, no one knew the secret except Sunday, "whose heart told her something was wrong."

Among the actors who were regulars on the series were Jay Jostyn who created the title role in radio's *Mr. District Attorney,* in the part of Jackie, and the late Van Heflin, who was Slim Delaney. While playing Sunday, Vivian Smolen moonlighted, often, as Lolly Baby on NBC's soaper "Stella Dallas."[3]

When the program went off the air on January 2, 1959, Sunday's last ordeal had come to a happy end, and she and Henry went off to England on a permanent vacation. Miss Smolen remembers the atmosphere in the studio was very depressing. But the cast and crew had developed strong friendships over the years and, of course, their salaries were steady and quite good.

Vivian got over her melancholy immediately when she married TV executive Harold Klein within weeks after the last broadcast. They live in Manhattan's east nineties in the same building with Mary Jane Higby, radio's Nora Drake and the key character for years on radio's "When a Girl Marries."

In the last two years she has appeared on TV commercials (Ivory soap, Phillip's milk of magnesia) that run frequently on the networks. Not long ago an interviewer who asked Vivian the question her program asked every day: "Can this girl from a mining town in the West find happiness as the wife of a wealthy and titled Englishman?" received the reply: "If Sunday had ever found happiness, several million women would have put down their irons and turned the dial."

In her New York City apartment recently. *Coleen Magee*

With Georgia Carrol shortly after their marriage, 1944.

KAY KYSER

The once popular band leader was born on June 18, 1906, in Rocky Mount, North Carolina, to the first registered woman pharmacist in the state. His father, who was almost totally blind, also practiced pharmacy. His real name is James Kern Kyser.

In both high school and college Kay was class president, editor of the yearbook, and cheerleader and coach of the football team. While at the University of North Carolina he also found time to organize a band that soon developed such a reputation that they were playing school dances in neighboring states. However, on their first playdate, 1926, Kay was so nervous he was unable to lead the group. The baton had to be taken over by his old friend, Johnny Mercer.

After a few lean years after college, Kyser opened at Chicago's famed Black Hawk Restaurant in September 1934, with a group called "Kay Kyser's Kampus Klass." It was soon changed to "Kay Kyser's Kollege of Musical Knowledge." But by that time the group had made a big hit not only with the club's audiences but on the regional radio network that carried the bands from the Black Hawk.

The Kyser sound was much like his idols', Fred Waring and Guy Lombardo, but Kay's group had much more class than the other Mickey Mouse type bands that merely imitated the giants. His boys stayed with him year after year and had a reputation for being well dressed and groomed. They got along so well that one of the complaints most often heard was that there was too much nonsense going on during songs like "Praise the Lord and Pass the Ammunition" and "Who Wouldn't Love You?," two of their biggest hits. However, the jokes and kidding worked well for the novelty numbers, which were their specialty.

Kyser's theme from the very beginning was "Thinking of You." Some of his vocalists were Ish Kabibble, the King Sisters, Ginny Simms,[3] Harry Babbitt (now the manager of the Newport Beach Tennis Club in California), and Mike Douglas, who was then known as Michael Douglas.

He and his band appeared in such feature films as *You'll Find Out* (1940), *My Favorite Spy* (1942), and *Swing Fever* (1943). His musical-quiz radio program was popular throughout the 1940s, during which time he played at 580 U.S. military installations around the world. In March of 1950 the program moved to NBC television. Kay always wore the traditional cap and gown, as did his musicians. The show's contestants had to answer his true or false questions, but with an incorrect answer. If they gave the correct answer, Kay would say, "That's right. You're wrong!" Incorrect answers drew "That's wrong. You're right!" Questions that couldn't be answered were referred to the studio audience by Kyser, who would shout, "Students?"

The man who musicologist George Simon once referred to as "a luscious ear in the field of corn" called it quits in 1954, when he turned over his TV hosting chores to Tennessee Ernie Ford.

Eleven years earlier he had married his songstress Georgia Carroll, a former John Powers model. The couple live in a 155-year-old house in Chapel Hill, North Carolina. Kay is a teacher and practitioner of Christian Science. One daughter is married and the two others attend Kay's alma mater. Kay has turned down interviews and very lucrative offers to return to TV with the same reply: "Those were wonderful years but they are long over. My concerns today are with my family and my faith."

A fan who recently brought around some of Kyser's old movies to show him said that the girls were not a bit interested in seeing them and that it seemed Kay and Georgia watched only out of politeness.

Mr. and Mrs. at home in Chapel Hill, North Carolina. *Milo Holt*

With Kay Kyser in a scene from *Playmates* (1941).

ISH KABIBBLE

Bandleader Kay Kyser's vocalist-comic was born in northeastern Pennsylvania on January 19, 1908, and raised in Erie where his father was a building contractor. His real name is Merwyn A. Bogue. At twelve he began to take lessons in piano and trumpet, playing both instruments throughout his high school years and also while attending West Virginia University. He majored in economics and pre-law but his real ambition, when he graduated in 1930, was to "sing like Bing Crosby."

The Depression was well underway in 1930 and when Kay Kyser offered him a job, at a low salary, doing just about everything but sweeping the floor, he grabbed it. Ish had a fair singing voice and was quite proficient on the trumpet, but in the early lean years he booked the band's hotel reservations, was responsible for their tickets, and anything else that had to be looked after. "We played for a couple of years," he reminisced recently, "and then one day Kay called the boys around and we decided we'd better do something if we were ever going to amount to anything." One of the things they felt they needed was a comedian. Jerry Colonna[3] advised them that whoever the guy was he needed a gimmick. Ish decided that if Colonna could convulse the audience with a mustache, he would be "the guy with the haircut." In those days no man would be caught dead wearing his hair in bangs. When audiences saw him they chuckled, and when he sang such songs as "Foodledy Racky-Sacky" or "Three Little Fishes" they howled. The record he made of "Fishes" sold over 5 million copies and started the non-

96

sense-song craze that lasted for years in the music business. He is also responsible for much of the success of one of the silliest songs ever—"Mairzy Doats."

His ridiculous name, which became a household word, came from the expression "ish," a sound used by musicians to convey the thought, "I should worry . . . ?" Kyser had asked him to think up a silly name just before their first broadcast over WGN; they were broadcasting live from Chicago's Black Hawk Restaurant, and Ish Kabibble was how he was introduced.

Ish was probably the most popular member of Kyser's "Kollege of Musical Knowledge," as they were billed, and was with him until the bandleader retired in 1952. Ish was featured in all the movies the group made, such as *That's Right—You're Wrong* (1939), *Playmates* (1941), and *Carolina Blues* (1944).

Ish Kabibble had a freedom in comedy that very few performers ever knew. He allowed himself to try anything and everything that he thought up or anyone suggested because throughout his public years he knew that his rich aunt (then worth $4½ million) was leaving everything to him. "I did as I pleased," says Ish today, "and do you know that my aunt lived to be 95 and spent every cent of that money before she went. God bless her. She must have had a ball."

Since leaving show business he has spent most of his time dealing in some phase of real estate. He worked for a while with Ginny Simms[3] on her land development project in the California desert, then spent some time in Seattle before a venture took him for a couple of years to Australia. He and his wife, whom he married in 1932, settled in Houston, Texas, until World Marketing offered him a job as a real estate salesman in Honolulu in 1972. Ish keeps his hair at the perfect length by combing it forward into his famous bangs just to reassure a potential client who, after accepting Ish's business card, asks, "What do you mean, Sales Manager: Ish Kabibble?"

During a recent, very rare TV appearance. *CBS-TV*

BEULAH BONDI

The distinguished character actress who was born Beulah Bondy on May 3, 1892, in Chicago, debuted at the age of seven in the title role of *Little Lord Fauntleroy*. By the time she was ten, her acting had won a gold medal.

Stuart Walker, then head of one of the country's leading repertory companies, signed her at $25 a week, but after two years she left to tour with various stock productions. In 1925 she debuted on Broadway in *One in the Family*. After a couple more plays she won the part of the landlady in the original company of *Street Scene* (1929) and was signed by Samuel Goldwyn to repeat the part in his film version (1931). She returned to Broadway only four more times: for *The Late Christopher Bean* (1932), *Mother Lode* (1934), *Hilda Crane* (1950), and *On Borrowed Time* (1953), which she had first done in a 1939 film version.

Beulah Bondi differs from other character actresses in several respects. She was never under contract and therefore was never forced to accept parts she felt were unsuitable. This also worked well for her financially: when producers wanted her they had to pay her price, which was $500 a week even in 1931. Her art was not in tricks, scene-stealing, or a flamboyant personality indigenous to her every role. She was a totally different person in every one of her 63 feature films. Today when people recognize her in public as one of the warm, cruel, or eccentric women she has portrayed in movies and not as an actress, she is paid the ultimate compliment.

Her more important films were *Arrowsmith* (1931), *Rain* (1932), with William Gargan (living in Rancho La Costa, California), *The Sisters* (1938), with Jane Bryan (married and living in Bel Air, California) and Ian Hunter (retired to Spain), *Mr. Smith Goes to Washington* (1939), with Jean Arthur (teaching drama at Vassar College), *Watch on the Rhine* (1943), *Our Hearts Were Young and Gay* (1944), with the late Diana Lynn, *The Southerner* (1945), with the late J. Carrol Naish, *The Snake Pit* (1948), with Glenn Langan (living with his wife, Adele Jergens, in Encino, California), and *Our Town* (1949). She made mediocre as well as bad pictures but her work in them was always of top quality. A few that appeared on television are *Two Alone* (1934), with Tom Brown (a regular on ABC-TV's "General Hospital") and Jean Parker (living in Glendale, California), *The Buccaneer* (1938), with Franceska Gaal (the late Mrs. Francis de Dajkovich of Manhattan), *The Under-Pup* (1939), with the late Virginia Weidler, *High Conquest* (1947), with Anna Lee (married to novelist Robert Nathan and living in Los Angeles), *So Dear to My Heart* (1948), with the late Bobby Driscoll, and *Latin Lovers* (1953), with John Lund (a Beverly Hills businessman who refuses to discuss his career). Her last screen appearance was in *Tammy and the Doctor* (1963), with Margaret Lindsay (living in West Hollywood).

Beulah has no regrets about not winning an Oscar for *The Gorgeous Hussy* (1936) or *Of Human Hearts* (1938), both nominated, but she was deeply disappointed when after several days of shooting she was replaced by May Robson in *The Adventures of Tom Sawyer* (1938). (Miss Robson, who was the original choice, recovered sooner than expected from an illness.) The real hurt came when the role of Ma Joad in *The Grapes of Wrath* (1940) was awarded to Jane Darwell after Beulah had been told it was hers.

Beulah has never been married and she lives alone in a beautiful old three-story house built into the face of the Hollywood Hills. Her home is filled with mementos not of her screen career but from the many countries she has visited during her two trips around the world. Africa fascinates her so much she has been there four times and she is planning a visit to the Soviet Union.

She had appeared on television very infrequently in the past ten years, and the only film role that has even tempted her was the part that won an Oscar for Helen Hayes in *Airport* (1970). Although Beulah has worked with such stars as Claudette Colbert (living in St. James, Barbados), Bette Davis, Barbara Stanwyck, Clark Gable, and Joan Crawford, Beulah was never a part of the Hollywood social scene, and none of her friends are movie people. Nor is she as old as people expect (as a young girl she did not play ingenues but went right into older roles).

She told an interviewer recently: "I have a very good, full life away from the stage and studios. I don't rule out working again but I don't have to either for my bank account or my ego. I feel very fulfilled."

The character actress with her close friend, classical tenor Charles Whitewolf. *Marion Weinstein*

As the mother in *Of Human Hearts* (1938). The role required her to age twenty years for the final scene.

In 1929, when he was staging the shows at New York's famed Capitol Theatre.

CHESTER HALE

The choreographer of stage, screen, and ice shows was born in Jersey City, New Jersey, on January 15, 1897. His father was a star reporter on the *New York Sun*.

Chester was always athletic but when he came to New York City one summer day in 1915 he was planning to be a doctor or to get into physical culture work. Then he saw some beautiful Leon Boch posters announcing the coming engagement of the Ballet Russe de Monte Carlo. Although he knew nothing about dance, he felt like joining the company and proceeded to the Grand Central Palace, where the troupe was rehearsing. After being auditioned by the legendary Nijinsky, he was hired to dance at $25 a week. Chester became a particular favorite of the premier danseur, who he remembers as a man with a terrible persecution complex. But during the fifty-five city tour, Chester discovered that Nijinsky's fears were quite real for he was envied and despised within the company for his amazing talent. After two years Chester left the company, which was under the direction of Diaghilev, to join Anna Pavlova's troupe in Buenos Aires.

When he returned to the United States, he landed a role in *As You Were* (1920) on Broadway and then a featured spot in the *Music Box Revue* of 1921, which took him on a United States tour and then to London. There, for the first time, for the *Revue,* he staged the dances. He became the first dancer for producer Charles B. Cochran, who encouraged him to work at choreography.

Many of his contemporaries thought he had cheapened himself when he gave up classical ballet for Broadway but he thoroughly enjoyed being in shows and found that he got even more satisfaction from training dancers. Increasingly he was staging numbers in such productions as *Greenwich Village Follies* (1928) and *Murder at the Vanities* (1933). The late Irene

Castle engaged him to stage her vaudeville act that toured the nation during the twenties. By the time he last danced before an audience, on the stage of the Capitol Theatre in 1928, with Hilde Butzova, he was the house's choreographer. He later produced its famed stage shows as well, under the supervision of Major Bowes. His Chester Hale Girls were internationally famous for their beauty and precision wherever they appeared, including the Dorchester in London and the Lido in Venice as well as the top presentation houses throughout the country.

M-G-M brought him to Hollywood for two frustrating years. He chafed under the studio's interference with his work but managed to stage dance numbers in several movies, including *A Night at the Opera* (1935) and *Rose Marie* (1936). His greatest pleasure and credit was teaching Greta Garbo the mazurka for *Anna Karenina* (1935).

Though Hale's choreography was quite different from contemporary Busby Berkeley's,[3] he was just as important and his services came high. Hale once charged R-K-O $1,000 to coach Lucille Ball in a single number. His Chester Hale Dance Studio in New York City was *the* place to learn what was needed to break into a Broadway chorus line during the twenties, thirties and forties. Sixty-four of his Chester Hale Girls were the hit of the Dallas Centennial of 1938, and he is credited with giving Alice Faye, Jessie Matthews,[1] and the late Miriam Hopkins their first breaks as chorus girls. Sally Rand[1] came to him when she needed money for her act that made show business history at the Chicago World's Fair of 1932–33.

During the 1940s and '50s Hale spent most of his time staging and directing thirteen editions of Ice Capades and then another thirteen of Holiday on Ice, traveling with the latter to their 1959 engagement in Moscow. Thereafter he retired.

Still very dapper, Chester and his wife, Marine, a former dancer he married in 1940, live in an apartment in Redondo Beach, California, where they spend a lot of time enjoying the ocean and weather while complaining about the dullness of Southern Californians. Chester has a son and three grandchildren.

With Marine Hale, in retirement, Redondo Beach, California. *David Heeley*

When "Vaya Con Dios" was the No. 1 record in the country for eleven weeks in the fall of 1953.

LES PAUL AND MARY FORD

The guitarist who introduced and perfected echo sound and multiple-track recordings was born in Waukesha, Wisconsin, on June 9, 1916. Les was a musician at fourteen, playing a Sears, Roebuck harmonica on radio station WRJN in Racine, Wisconsin. Graduating to guitar, he worked in Chicago and New York for seven years in a hillbilly act, "Rhubarb Red," before moving around as a sideman for Fred Waring, Benny Goodman, Art Tatum, and Ben Bernie.

In the 1940s the Les Paul Trio was heard on the "Burns and Allen Show" on radio and on recordings for Decca and Capitol. Paul had a reputation among his peers as one of the best guitarists in the business and the Les Paul Electric Guitar he developed is still the largest-selling stringed instrument in the country. But he was far from content. He complained constantly about recording techniques, which he felt were inadequate. (Bing Crosby once said to him: "Les, why don't you just build your own studio?")

Playing Chicago's Oriental Theatre, his trio, with their jazz numbers, was well received. But it was the headliners, the Andrews Sisters,[3] who were bringing down the house. And when shortly after that his own mother confused his playing on radio with another guitarist, that did it. Paul disbanded the trio, notified his agent that he would accept no more jobs until further notice, and holed up for the next two years in his garage, experimenting with tape recorders.

He tried to record his new sound with Kay Starr, but it just didn't jell. Then Eddie Dean, Jimmy's brother, told him about Colleen Summers, who was vocalist on Gene Autry's Sunday night radio program.

Colleen (born in Pasadena, California, on July 7, 1924) had specialized in country and western music with Jimmy Wakely and on "Hollywood Barndance" with Mike Douglas. Paul changed her style, informed her she was "flat," and rehearsed her until she hardly knew her name—since he changed it to Mary Ford—and, in 1949, he married her.

The first Les Paul and Mary Ford disc, "Lover," was released by Capitol in 1949 and within weeks was on top of the charts. It was the first of their twenty-one hits in a row. Paul took standards like "Mockin'bird Hill," "The World Is Waiting for the Sunrise," and "Just One More Chance" and made them sound totally new with his use of echo and multiple-track recording. A new generation ate up his renditions of "Bye, Bye, Blues" and "Nola," while parents rediscovered their old favorites like "Tiger Rag" and "Caravan." They were so hot their single "How High the Moon" was the No. 1 record in the country from April 21 to June 16, 1951. Les and Mary considered their cover record of Patti Page's hit, "Tennessee Waltz," a disappointment when it sold only 800,000 copies.

The duo was still on top with TV, nightclub, and White House appearances when the story of their divorce broke across the country. Within hours of the news the commercials they had recorded for Robert Hall clothes were, at the insistence of the sponsor, taken off radio stations.

Mary worked in an act with her family for a while until a financial settlement was reached and then married Don Hatfield, a contractor who was her boyfriend in high school. In the final settlement, Mary got custody of their son and daughter while Les took their collection of gold records, plus the platinum one they received for their 4-million seller "Vaya Con Dios."

Thereafter, Les didn't pick up a guitar in eight years and even now plays only as a favor to musician friends when their guitarist can't make an engagement.

Les has not remarried and still lives in the huge house in Mahwah, New Jersey, he and Mary occupied during the peak years. It is full of complicated recording equipment, much of which he invented.

Les and Mary are on speaking terms now and see each other when he is on the West Coast. Mary lives with her husband in Monrovia, California, on enough land to accommodate a large family and three horses. She would like to work again but never at the pace Les insisted on. One thing she and Les agree on is that even if the harmony hadn't gone out of their marriage they would have lost interest in the kind of music that made them famous and rich. However, Les is now considering forming a group of youngsters.

The inventor-bachelor-multimillionaire at WBAI-FM studios in New York. *Paul Schaeffer*

Mary is now Mrs. Hatfield of Monrovia, California. *Ian Hayes*

INGEMAR JOHANSSON

The former Heavyweight Boxing Champion of the World was born on September 22, 1932, in Gotëborg, Sweden. As a boy he was constantly in fights and left school when he was fifteen to work as a street laborer and dock worker.

He was inspired by the stories his stonecutter father used to tell about their cousin Ring Larson, who had a good boxing career during the 1930s in the United States as a lightweight.

Ingo, as the sportswriters later dubbed him, began to train for a ring career when he was thirteen years old. Soon a Swedish magazine publisher-sports promoter took an interest in him, and by 1947 Ingemar was being taken seriously as an amateur. In 1948 he became Junior Champion of his hometown and then spent fifteen months in the Swedish navy. In 1950 he was proclaimed Sweden's Heavyweight Champion and in 1951 entered the Golden Gloves competition in Chicago where he KO'd Ernest Fann.

He entered the 1952 Olympics in Helsinki and was kissed and booed when he was eliminated from competition for not fighting. The *New York Herald Tribune* called him frightened, and in his native land headlines screamed "Ingemar, For Shame!" His showing had been so poor that the judges would not grant him second place, which he technically rated, and the customary silver medal was denied him.

Ingemar has said of the incident that he was only obeying his advisers' orders, which were to take it easy and allow his opponent to reveal himself. It was a very black mark on his record and only his amazing showing afterward obscured it. He won 21 fights in a row, 12 by KOs. By 1958 he had become the first European since Max Schmeling[1] to be named Fighter of the Year.

Yet when he stepped into the ring with Floyd Patterson on June 26, 1959, he had everything against him, except his good looks. He was a 5 to 1 underdog, a foreigner, and he had trained while living with his fiancée, all the time making the rounds of New York night spots and talk shows. He told everyone who would listen about his right hand, which he said had about it "something mystic." It may have at that because after two minutes and three seconds of the third round Floyd Patterson was on the canvas and the world had a new Heavyweight Champion.

He was exactly what the scandal-ridden sport needed. Patterson, a fine fighter, seemed dull even to his fans. Ingemar wore his crown with great style, cavorting around New York and Hollywood with stars like Peggy Lee, Stella Stevens, and Farley Granger (now living in Rome). He sang songs on Dinah Shore's program, starred in the movie *All the Young Men* (1960), and appeared on most of the TV panel and talk shows (on one he dressed up like Greta Garbo).

By the time of the rematch on March 13, 1961, the right hand had become known as "the Hammer of Thor," but in the sixth round Patterson knocked him out, thus becoming the first Heavyweight Champion in history to regain the title.

Ingemar, however, kept right on fighting and not only won every one of his bouts after that, but on June 17, 1962, took the European heavyweight crown. After defeating Brian London on April 21, 1963, he retired.

Johansson resides in Gotëborg, although he spends much of the year in Switzerland. He has had some bad press over tax troubles and drinking bouts, and also over the divorce from his second wife, Birgit Lundgren, but he is still very popular in Sweden. His father kept a close watch on Ingemar's earnings, and his investments in land have made him a very wealthy man. Ingemar is a major partner in Swedish bingo interests (bingo is a fad there) which has proved very profitable. Not too long ago he told some reporters that he was thinking of making a comeback. The newsmen, spotting the ex-champ's enormous stomach, could only chalk it off as one of the put-ons Ingemar loved to indulge in during his salad days.

With British heavyweight Henry Cooper (left), weighing in for their 1957 bout. *UPI*

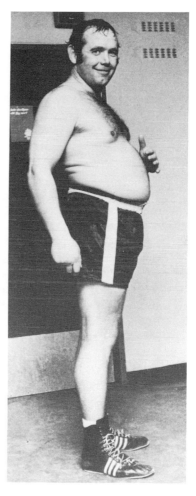

At 265 pounds in a recent workout. *Wide World*

Mae takes a blow for male chauvinism in the famous scene from *Public Enemy* (1931).

MAE CLARKE

The promising leading lady of the 1930s was born Mary Klotz in Philadelphia, Pennsylvania, on August 16, 1910. Her father was a theatre organist, well known in his area, and Mae got to see lots of free movies as a little girl. Her idol was Richard Dix.

As a child she took interpretive dancing and at the age of thirteen began performing in nightclubs. By fourteen she was one of May Dawson's Dancing Girls. In 1924 producer Earl Lindsay saw her and put her in a show performed on the roof of the Strand Theatre in New York City. From there Mae went into small roles in such musicals as *The Noose* (1926) and *Manhattan Mary* (1927). After a vaudeville tour, Fox Pictures brought her and Lee Tracy to Hollywood to star in *Big Time* (1929). After that she worked with Lois Moran (Mrs. Clarence Young of Palo Alto, California) in *The Dancers* (1930).

It is difficult to understand why she never became a major star after 1931, even if only for a while. She played Molly, the prostitute, in *The Front Page,* a smash hit of the period. She had the female lead in the classic *Frankenstein* and starred in *Waterloo Bridge* with the late Douglass Montgomery, who worked then as Kent Douglass. The production, which had Bette Davis billed seventh, has not been shown in years because of the remakes. However, it was one of the most coveted assignments in Hollywood, and her notices were excellent. That same year, she appeared in a scene that may have made her a movie immortal and/or ruined her career. The picture was *Public Enemy,* in which she had only two scenes. In one, she breakfasted with her boyfriend, Jimmy Cagney, who then insults her. The director, William Wellman, yelled "Cut." Wellman then asked if she would do another take "for a laugh," only this time Cagney was not going to tell her to shut up but instead would shove a grapefruit in her face. "I've always tried to be a good sport," she says. "The idea didn't appeal to me. Nobody likes having anything pushed into her face but since it was only a gag I consented." She went home and forgot about it. When the picture was released she was astonished to find that the second version was in it. The press had a field day. Women's rights groups raised hell. The scene, and the picture's success, is credited by many people as triggering the abuse of women. Anyway, the abuse followed in many of the films thereafter.

Mae worked a lot after that in such movies as *Nana* (1934), with Anna Sten,[1] *Hats Off* (1937), with John Payne,[3] *Women in War* (1940), with Wendy Barrie (living in Manhattan), *Sailors on Leave* (1941), with William Lundigan (living in Beverly Hills), *Kitty* (1945), with Paulette Goddard,[1] and *Annie Get Your Gun* (1950). Because she is well liked around the studios, she has never stopped acting completely. But her parts are small and her fine work of the early years is remembered only by film buffs who watch for her in *The Great Caruso* (1951), *Singin' in the Rain* (1952), *Voice in the Mirror* (1958) and *Thoroughly Modern Millie* (1967). When she signed for a part in *Water Melon Man* (1970), she was asked to pose for publicity stills with Godfrey Cambridge in which he would threaten her with a grapefruit. "So, what the hell, I went along with the gag," she says philosophically.

Between her bit parts, and TV roles, she paints. Mae lives alone in a small apartment in North Hollywood. Though it's been years since she last heard from her former friend Barbara Stanwyck, who started with her in chorus lines during the 1920s, she and Cagney occasionally exchange notes. One of her close pals is Robert Arthur, who now runs an acting school. Mae hasn't been lucky either in money or love. "I was paid the same as others at the time but I never really made big money. Certainly not enough to save." Her second and third marriages (an airline pilot and an army captain) ended in divorce, as did her first, to Lew Brice, brother of Fanny Brice. "He hated being known as Mr. Mae Clarke, poor guy. But what man wouldn't?"

Beside a painting she completed recently. *Jack Sigesmund*

In 1961 when Twentieth Century-Fox Studios was giving Richard the big publicity buildup.

RICHARD BEYMER

The Hollywood dreamboat of the 1950s was born on February 21, 1939, in Avoca, Iowa, and baptized George Richard Beymer, Jr. His father, a printer, brought the family to Los Angeles when Richard was nine years old. Even before arriving in the movie capital, Richard was fascinated by motion pictures. And when he learned that the older boy next door went to dance class, he convinced his parents that he too should be allowed to take lessons.

By 1952 he was a regular on a live Saturday night show on the pioneer Los Angeles TV station KTLA; "Sandy's Dream," later known as "Fantastic Studios" was about a group of kids who pretended they were making motion pictures. Richard was paid $8 every week, and loved every minute of it.

Vittorio De Sica picked Beymer (pronounced Bee-mer) from a line of several hundred boys who auditioned for the part of Jennifer Jones's nephew in *Indiscretion of an American Wife* (1954) —mainly because his complexion was similar to the star's. David O. Selznick put him under contract for a year and he was promptly loaned out to Warner Brothers for *So Big* (1953), which was made after *Indiscretion* but released before.

After making *Johnny Tremain* (1957) for Disney, he was placed under contract to Twentieth Century-Fox, which had big plans for him as one of their new faces. The publicity department went to work to make him into an idol of teen-agers throughout the world.

After playing Millie Perkins's boyfriend in *The Diary of Anne Frank* (1959) and appearing with Bing Crosby in *High Time* (1960), Beymer was considered a very hot property. Warners wanted him for the title role in *Parrish* which eventually went to Troy Donahue. Instead Fox gave him the plum part opposite Natalie Wood in *West Side Story* (1961), and then the vehicle *Bachelor Flat* (1961).

How Richard got the part in *West Side Story* is still a mystery. Every young actor on both coasts wanted to do it, and some of them could sing.

Beymer's songs had to be dubbed. He admits that when he finally saw himself on the screen during the last days of shooting he was "very shaken" and that his knees buckled. The audiences and critics who saw him in the picture merely winced.

He made *The Longest Day* (1962), *Five Finger Exercise* (1962), and had a splendid chance to redeem himself as the star of *Hemingway's Adventures of a Young Man* (1962), but again turned in a performance that has been called everything from disappointing to embarrassing. Fox did not pick up his option at the seventh year.

Richard took the advice of Joanne Woodward, with whom he worked in *The Stripper* (1963), and went to New York where he studied at Actors Studio. In 1964 he was part of the drive to register black voters in Mississippi. He made a documentary about it, which has been well received at a few film festivals. Thereafter he spent some time in London trying, without success, to establish himself as a filmmaker.

In the mid-sixties he was seen on a few TV shows, including "The Man from U.N.C.L.E."

He sees no one from the old days and recently, in a restaurant, when he spoke to Joanne Woodward and Paul Newman they at first found it difficult to believe he was really Richard Beymer. He goes about unrecognized in the city that once hailed him as a new star. Nor do the movie and TV people who work out in the same gym with him know who he is, or else they don't care.

Richard is unmarried and lives alone (less than a block from Paramount Studios) in an apartment that could more accurately be described as a pad. The building bears a large plaque commemorating its onetime tenant Jack London. In Richard's rooms are the strips of film from the feature he has been working on for some time. He describes it as "the pictures in my mind."

Beymer is amused by people who look on his career as a failure. "I don't need that white Corvette anymore," he says. "In fact, I never did need it but I was foolish enough to want it. Everything I need I've got. It's all within me."

A very different Richard today on his terrace in Hollywood. *Michael Knowles*

In *Topper Returns* (1941), where the script required Eddie to kiss a seal.

"ROCHESTER": Eddie Anderson

The actor who became a household name through his portrayal of Jack Benny's valet was born on September 18, 1905, in Oakland, California. His parents, Big Ed and Ella Mae, worked as aerialists in circuses and on the vaudeville circuits. When Eddie was twelve years old his voice left him completely after a day of hawking newspapers on a San Francisco street corner. When it returned it had the scratchy quality that years later would bring him success on radio.

In the twenties, Eddie worked in vaudeville as one of the "Three Black Aces," along with his brother Cornelius, and toured with the California Collegians, a band that included an unknown Fred MacMurray. Eddie also worked at the Cotton Club for two and a half years, six nights a week.

After working around Los Angeles in nightclubs, he debuted in movies in *What Price Hollywood* (1932), which was the original version of *A Star Is Born*. He was in *Three Men on a Horse* (1936) with Frank McHugh (living in Cos Cob, Connecticut), *Green Pastures* (1936), playing the character Noah, *Melody for Two* (1937), with Sally Blane,[3] *Gold Diggers in Paris* (1938), with Rosemary Lane (now a real estate dealer in Pacific Palisades, California), and as Uncle Peter in *Gone With the Wind* (1939).

His first appearance (after he auditioned for Benny) as Rochester Van Jones, a Pullman porter on Benny's Sunday night radio program, was on Easter Sunday, 1937. Benny liked Eddie's distinctive voice and felt he would register with radio audiences. Soon Anderson had a running part as Benny's valet and the Van Jones was dropped. One of his duties was to look after Carmichael, the polar bear Benny kept in the basement to guard his vault. From time to time Rochester would make references to the gas man Carmichael was supposed to have devoured. The character continued to appear almost every week right into the 1950s and was featured on many of Benny's TV shows as well. His popularity at one point brought two thousand letters a week; this was NBC's figure, and while no one disputed the count, little was said about some of the audience's disapproval of the characterization. Many listeners were particularly offended by Eddie addressing Benny as *Boss*.

If Anderson ever objected to the stereotype casting, on the air and in films, it was done very quietly; certainly nothing came of it because he continued to play the chauffeur, factory worker, or janitor. By 1940 he was so identified with the radio character, he was even billed as Rochester on film credits, and not only in the Jack Benny vehicles *Buck Benny Rides Again* (1940) and *The Meanest Man in the World* (1943), with Priscilla Lane (Mrs. Joseph A. Howard of Derry, New Hampshire). Some of Rochester's other pictures are *Cabin in the Sky* (1943), *Brewster's Millions* (1945), *The Sailor Takes a Wife* (1945), and *The Show-Off* (1947). He was also often part of the stage presentation at New York's famous Roxy Theatre, as well as at the Apollo Theatre in Harlem.

The fifties brought change. In 1952 his son Willie was given a suspended sentence for possession of marijuana, in 1954 his wife, Mamie, died of cancer, and two years later son Willie, who had become an outstanding athlete in school and for a while was a professional football player with the Chicago Bears, was sentenced to five years in prison for the sale and possession of marijuana. And Rochester figured less and less in the Benny shows. During rehearsals for a Benny TV show in 1958, Eddie suffered a heart attack from which he has never completely recovered. The recent difficulty he has had with his sight and speech have further curtailed professional engagements. But as the new image of the black man emerged, Eddie had further submerged. His appearance in *It's a Mad, Mad, Mad, Mad World* (1963) was his first since 1947, and his last.

Three Anderson children, by his second wife, whom he married in 1956, live with the couple in the largest house on a dead-end street in a fashionable black neighborhood in Los Angeles. Almost daily during racing season Eddie can be found at the track, and he is often accompanied by his old friend Jack Benny. Eddie is delighted to oblige fans with autographs, signing them "Rochester."

With Edmond Anderson on the grounds of their Los Angeles home. *Chris Albertson*

By the early forties one of the most popular leading men in Hollywood.

GEORGE BRENT

The popular leading man of movies was born George B. Nolan in Shannonsbridge, Ireland, on March 3, 1904. After his parents died in 1915 he lived for a while in New York City. But he returned to Ireland, where he became a dispatch carrier for the IRA leader Michael Collins. Collins was killed and the British had put out a reward for Brent's capture, so he left for the United States. In Dublin he had managed to spend some time with the Abbey Players, and now he toured the country in *Abie's Irish Rose,* in 1925. He then opened two little theatres, one in Rhode Island and one in Florida, but both failed. He did *The K-Guy* (1928), *Those We Love* (1930), and *Love, Honor and Betray* (1930). The latter got Hollywood interested. He did six features but not before *The Rich Are Always With Us* (1932) did he click: Warner Brothers signed him, the public noticed him, and the picture's star, Ruth Chatterton (at the time the First Lady of the Screen), married him. In the picture, Brent put two cigarettes in his mouth, lit both, and handed one to Ruth. Ten years later Paul Henreid created a minor sensation and a fad among couples, when he did the same thing for Bette Davis in *Now, Voyager.* Miss Davis had played a small role in *The Rich Are Always With Us.*

Brent was a ladies' man and his studio made the most of it. He dressed impeccably (but was never a fop), spoke beautifully, and had an air that suggested he would stand only for so much nonsense. The quality was a good foil to the antics of his leading ladies. It gave them some sense of reality. Women may have gone to the movies to see their stars Kay Francis, Greta Garbo, Bette Davis, Barbara Stanwyck, and Hedy Lamarr but they left to dream about George who handled all the female neuroses with charm and firmness.

Brent's screen image was that of the marrying kind of man, and it wasn't far off in real life. Preceding his career, he had been married briefly in 1922 to an unknown actress; then after two years as "Mr. Ruth Chatterton," he was married to Constance Worth for under a year, and from 1942 to 1943 he was married to the late Ann Sheridan. Many people speculated that George is the unnamed love in Bette Davis's autobiography. He costarred in eleven of her films.

In spite of his popularity not one of the eighty-four movies he played in was "his" picture. Among them were *Desirable* (1934), with Verree Teasdale (the widow of Adolphe Menjou lives in Beverly Hills), *Living on Velvet* (1935), *Jezebel* (1938), *The Rains Came* (1939), *Dark Victory* (1939), his favorite, *The Great Lie* (1940), *The Gay Sisters* (1942), with Larry Simms (the actor who became famous as "Baby Dumpling" works at the Jet Propulsion Lab in Pasadena), *The Spiral Staircase* (1946), *Red Canyon* (1949), and his last, *Mexican Manhunt* (1953). For years after his retirement he raised horses, but he has given that up.

His fifth marriage, to an artist, has produced two girls and a boy. The couple live in a big house in exclusive Rancho Santa Fe, California.

Although he almost never hears from his contemporaries nor sees new movies he does not rule out a comeback. He thinks he would be perfect for the Ernest Hemingway story if it is ever filmed. In the last few months, since he gave up his three-packs-a-day cigarette habit, he has gained thirty-eight pounds.

In the sun in Rancho Santa Fe, California. *Kendra Kerr*

After *Bad Girl,* one of the hottest stars under contract to Fox.

SALLY EILERS

The star of early talkies was born Dorothea Sallye Eilers to an Irish father and Jewish mother in New York City on December 11, 1908. She was in her early teens when because of her brother's health her family moved to Los Angeles.

Once there, Sally played hooky from Fairfax High School to visit the nearby studios, and began to get bit parts—with the help of her friend Carole Lombard who introduced her to Mack Sennett. By 1928 Sally had been named a Wampas Baby Star and made appearances in several features, including *Cradle Snatchers* (1927), followed by *Show of Shows* (1929) and *Dough Boys* (1930), with Buster Keaton. By then she was married to the popular western star Hoot Gibson and had been signed to a contract with Fox Films. Sally became leading lady to her husband in several movies and was with Spencer Tracy in his second film, *Quick Millions* (1931), in which she was billed third. One year later she got top billing over Tracy in *Disorderly Conduct* (1932)—which had followed *Bad Girl* (1931) and a resultant Oscar for the director and writer, and stardom for Sally. *Bad Girl* also launched a series of films Sally costarred in with the late James Dunn.

Sally was exceptionally good in *State Fair* (1933), but her wrong-side-of-the-track image ultimately kept her from growing. It was about this time that her marriage to Gibson ended, followed a month later by marriage to the late producer Harry Joe Brown.

Sally had an M-G-M contract, but her clashes with Louis B. Mayer, who disapproved of her salty language, didn't further her career. She worked often through the thirties and forties in such unimportant films as *Pursuit* (1935), with the late Chester Morris, *Remember the Night* (1935), with

Constance Cummings (one of the most popular stars on the London stage and married to playwright Ben Levy), *Condemned Women* (1938), with Louis Hayward (living in Palm Springs), *I Was a Prisoner on Devil's Island* (1941), *Strange Illusion* (1945), with Jimmy Lydon, and *Coroner Creek* (1948), with Margaret Chapman (living in Hollywood). She was last seen in *Stage to Tucson* (1950) with Rod Cameron (living in Malibu).

Sally has a son by Brown, from whom she got a friendly, financially profitable, divorce. Her third husband was a handsome naval officer, Howard Barney. Marriage No. 4 was to movie director John Hollingsworth Morse, who left her in 1958 and has been paying alimony ever since.

Even after Sally's career faded, she was a familiar face among Hollywood's social set. She had money, dressed well, and had a reputation for a quick, at times outrageous, wit. She had long ceased to be a big name, but she would pop up in Louella Parsons's column and had been a frequent guest at San Simeon. Sally was a particular favorite of Marion Davies', who relied on her for the latest off-color joke and gossip. Sally may have been the "bad girl" to her fans, but among film folk she was known as a good sport.

However, serious illness curtailed her partygoing for the last couple of years. She lives alone, except for her two Yorkies, in a small house in Beverly Hills overlooking a canyon right down the road from Rock Hudson's.

With one of her two Yorkies in Beverly Hills. *Martitia Palmer*

In 1935 Danilova danced *Nocturne,* choreographed by David Lichine, in London.

ALEXANDRA DANILOVA

The prima ballerina assoluta was born in Peterhof, Russia, on November 20, 1906. Her parents died when she was very young and Alexandra was reared by the wife of the Commander of the Imperial Armies of the Caucasus. When Alexandra at the age of eight played a butterfly in a Christmas play, everyone commented on her gracefulness. She had never seen a ballet but thereafter she begged to be allowed dancing lessons. Of 315 who applied at the Imperial Ballet School, she was one of seventeen accepted. Throughout her training period, Alexandra seemed destined for greatness and by more than one critic was called "the second Pavlova." After only a year, she was chosen to dance solo in *Coppélia.* Not even the Revolution affected her career. Immediately upon graduation from the Choreographic Technicum of Leningrad, she became a member of the corps de ballet of the Maryinsky Theatre. In her second year there, she was picked to dance the title role of *Firebird,* an unheard-of honor considering her experience and age. In the summer of 1922, with George Balanchine and Tamara Geva (single and living in Manhattan) she left the USSR for a state-approved tour of Western Europe. She never returned.

She was engaged by Serge Diaghilev, impresario of the Ballet Russe de Monte Carlo, and remained with his troupe until he died in 1929.

In 1932 she scored a great success in London in the operetta *Waltzes From Vienna.* Two years later she arrived, for the first time, in the United States.

During her long career, Danilova has danced with all the great males of the century: André Eglevsky,[3] Léonide Massine, Michel Fokine, Serge Lifar (living in Paris where he choreographs and teaches) and Igor Uskayvich.

Along with her extraordinary grace and precision, she had great versatility. She performed in diverse roles, in the classic tragedy *Odette* as well as the joyous *Petrouchka*. The one unfulfilled wish of her career was to dance the complete *Sleeping Beauty*, in which she was seen many times in the last act—the one and only act usually produced.

Danilova rejoined the Ballet Russe in 1938 and was their prima ballerina until 1951. However, she made many guest appearances, such as in 1949 with the Sadler's Wells Ballet, and in 1944 her dance was one of the highlights of the hit Broadway musical, *Song of Norway*. From 1954 to 1956, with her own company, Great Moments in Ballet, she toured North America, South Africa, and Asia.

The one sour note of Danilova's career was at the very end, when Sergei Demham, her impresario for a number of years, refused to give her a farewell performance. She still feels deeply about this breach of tradition and professional rudeness, but bid her public a memorable adieu on May 4, 1957, at the Metropolitan Opera House.

However, the next year she charmed Broadway audiences in the hit musical *Oh, Captain,* and has since then, in the fifties, staged for the Metropolitan such operas as *Boris Godunov, La Gioconda,* and *La Périchole.*

Madame Danilova, who lives alone, has since divided her time between her cottage in Lakewood, New Jersey, and a small apartment around the corner from Manhattan's City Center where she conducts classes several afternoons a week under the direction of her first husband, George Balanchine. Her second marriage, to a businessman, ended with his death and a third marriage, to a dancer, was annulled.

Madame Danilova in her Manhattan apartment. *Clayton Cole*

With Ole Olsen (*left*) and Chic Johnson in a scene from
Ghost Catchers (1944).

ELLA MAE MORSE

The Cow-Cow Boogie Girl was born in Mansfield, Texas, on September 12, 1925. By the time she was nine years old, Ella, with her mother at the piano, sang with her father's small band, appearing at lodge parties and school dances.

By 1939 her parents had separated, Ella had quit school, and her mother was working for $17 a week in an underwear factory. In 1939 Ella married Dick Showalter who led a small group under the name Dick Walters. Ella hung around the Adolphus Hotel, in Dallas, and tried to get a job with Phil Harris. He turned her down because of her age. The late Rudolf Friml also said no, as did Tommy Dorsey. But when Tommy's brother Jimmy came to town, Ella decided to say she was nineteen; her mother promised to back her up. She was hired at $100 a week and went with the Dorsey aggregation to their New Yorker Hotel engagement.

Ella had an excellent musical sense but was quite unprofessional and seemed to have no sense of what could or should be done on radio. She sang risqué lyrics and would announce on a coast-to-coast hookup that she had forgotten the words of a song.

Within a few weeks Dorsey found out about her age and she was replaced by Helen O'Connell.[3] Thereafter Ella sang in a Los Angeles ballroom for a while and then signed on with Freddie Slack, Dorsey's former pianist. Slack's newly formed band had a long engagement at the Pacific Square

Ballroom in San Diego.

But Ella didn't make it until she cut "Cow-Cow Boogie," one of the first records produced by the new company, Capitol, in 1942. The song had been done first by Ella Fitzgerald in a movie, but it landed on the cutting-room floor. Backed by Slack, Ella did it in one take, and although her contract called for a flat $35 fee Johnny Mercer later authorized that she be paid royalties on the million-plus seller. She followed it up with such hits as "Mister Five by Five," "House of Blue Lights," "Shoo Shoo, Baby," "No Love, No Nothin'," and "Milkman, Keep Those Bottles Quiet."

Ella was one of the nation's top vocalists during the big band era. She appeared with Charlie Barnett at the Strand Theatre in New York City and was seen in four movies: *Reveille with Beverly* (1943), *Ghost Catchers* (1944), with Lon Chaney, Jr. (living in Capistrano Beach, California), and Martha O'Driscoll (Mrs. Arthur Appleton of Chicago), *South of Dixie* (1944), and *How Do You Do* (1945), with Harry Von Zell (doing TV commercials in Los Angeles), and Bert Gordon, "the Mad Russian."[3]

Two years after a divorce from Showalter, in 1944, she married a doctor, a union that lasted until 1953. Five years later she married her present husband, Jack Bradford, a carpenter. In 1959, she recorded her last album, *The Morse Code,* with Billy May, but nothing much happened with it. Her sound was out during the fifties and sixties and she underwent a period of serious illness. In 1964 she was reportedly operating an elevator in Reno.

Ella and her family live in a small house in Hermosa Beach, California. The younger of her six children are teen-agers, and she feels now that she has the freedom and drive to work again. In 1972 she played several local dates and thoroughly enjoyed her reception. Encouraged by the nostalgia boom and Capitol's reissue of her "Cow-Cow Boogie" single, she is ready for a comeback. "The public never forgets you," she says. "I believe they'd love to see me back and I want them to know that I'm comin'."

Flanked by two of her six children. *Lawrence Orme*

Frankie's heyday was in the late thirties.

FRANKIE DARRO

The pint-sized actor was born Frank Johnson in Chicago on December 22, 1917. He accompanied his parents, as aerialists, on their tours with the Sells Brothers Circus, until his mother had a nervous breakdown during an engagement in Long Beach, California. His dad knew producer Ralph Ince and Frankie got a part in *Judgement of the Storm* (1923), with Wallace Beery. The family settled in Hollywood. Mr. Johnson was able to find considerable work as a stuntman, and Frankie performed in small parts in such films as *Cowboy Cop* (1926), with Jean Arthur (teaching drama at Vassar), and Frank Capra's *Paul Street Boys* (1929). For a time during the twenties Frankie was under contract to FBO, working with Tom Tyler. During the late days of the Depression, while playing vaudeville in Chicago, Frankie met and became engaged to a girl named Virginia who was part of a singing act called the Gumm Sisters. Neither the engagement nor the act lasted, but one of the sisters did—as Judy Garland.

Frankie was never a major star but he was the lead in a great many low-budget pictures. While under contract to Monogram during the thirties and forties he headed the cast of as many as seven features a month. If anyone was ever typecast Darro was. To this day Johnny Carson (who has never met him) constantly refers to him as always playing the jockey. He played the part not only in dozens of horseracing films made on his home lot but in such A products as Jean Harlow's last picture, *Saratoga* (1937). He was a jockey in *Broadway Bill* (1934) and again when it was remade for Bing Crosby as *Riding High* (1950). Two of his other better racing films were *Salty O'Rourke* (1945) and *Heart of Virginia* (1948).

Some of his best work was playing punks in such pictures as *Wild Boys of the Road* (1933) and *Reformatory* (1938). He was also in a few serials; one was Gene Autry's[1] *Phantom Empire* (1935). He was also in *Across the Wide Missouri* (1951) and *Operation Petticoat* (1959).

His top salary in his heyday was $1,750 a week. "I should have been paid by the mile," he says. He was so associated with horse racing that he is often kidded about having blown all his money at the track. The truth is that although he likes horses and rides very well, racing never interested him; he swears he can count the times he was at a track, except to shoot a scene.

For years Frankie had been a regular on TV's "Red Skelton Show," although very few fans would recognize him in drag, playing little old ladies taking the incredible pratfalls.

He is constantly recognized wherever he goes and admittedly enjoys it. "Except that they'll always ask you, 'Why don't we see you anymore, Frankie'?, and I got no answer for that." Considering that his chief source of income of late has been unemployment compensation, he takes the kidding and comments very well and is remarkably free of bitterness.

When he left for a USO tour of U.S. bases in Southeast Asia in 1970, his two-room apartment was full of patriotic posters. When he returned, he removed them. "I learned a lot I didn't know about what we've done over there. It's a dirty, filthy war and I want no more part of it," he said.

The only friends from the old days that he still sees are Mantan Moreland[3] and Jack Mulhall. Frankie and his former actress-wife Aloha Carroll—married since 1951, and introduced by Frankie's first wife, Aloha Wray, who committed suicide—live in upper Hollywood Boulevard in an old hotel inhabited mainly by pensioners and welfare recipients.

As he looks today. *Dick Lynch*

In June, 1956, leading Margaret Rinker on drums, Lois Cronin on trombone, and Helen Hammond on trumpet. *NBC*

INA RAY HUTTON

The lusty blonde bandleader was born in Chicago in 1917. By the time she was four years old she was dancing, and at five undertook piano lessons. When Ina was eight, her mother, Marvel Ray, took her to Chicago's State Theatre where Gus Edwards was auditioning children for his famous kiddie acts touring the vaudeville circuits. Out of a thousand boys and girls Edwards picked Ina.

In 1926 she played the Palace Theatre in *Gus Edwards' Future Stars.* All she remembers of the engagement is that she did a small bit with Bill "Bojangles" Robinson. She stayed with Edwards until she was twelve, when her mother decided it was time to book her as a single.

Ina was still being billed as Ina Ray when she got a part in the short-lived *Melody,* which George White produced, starring Hal Skelly, in 1933. From that Ina landed a featured role in the 1934 *Ziegfeld Follies,* which included Eve Arden, June Preisser (now living in Florida), and Brice Hutchins, who later became Bob Cummings.

The idea for Ina to lead an all-girl band came from Johnny Hyde, who headed the William Morris Agency. With his help, Ina put the band together in 1935, and it was a commercial success from the start. Musically, however, it was never taken seriously. Ina liked the band business very much but wanted her contribution to be more than a novelty act. Another drawback with the all-girl outfit was replacements. "I went crazy trying to get a female drummer on short notice even in New York," said Ina recently, "but when you're playing Milwaukee—forget it!"

By 1940 she was leading all men, and with the help of her boyfriend-arranger-manager George Paxton became a top attraction at such spots as the Palais Royale and the Paramount Theatre. Not only was the quality of the music infinitely better but the masculine background was perfect to set off Ina—a luscious blonde in a tight dress.

She made a short for Paramount in 1943, and Columbia starred her in a feature, *Ever Since Venus* (1944), with the late Billy Gilbert.[2] Her forte, however, was not acting but being herself.

She had disbanded her aggregation in 1947 and settled down to the quiet life in Los Angeles when Klaus Lansberg, the late television impresario, put her on Channel 5—again with an all-girl group. For the next five years her show was one of the top-rated local programs. During the summer of 1956 the Purex Company sponsored her nationally over NBC where she replaced "The $100,000 Big Surprise." There was serious talk of Ina continuing with her girls right through the year but NBC couldn't find a time slot that all parties could agree on; also she wasn't that enthusiastic about working hard again.

The last time the public saw the famous infectious smile, and the well-rounded body that moved a bit more than necessary, was in 1960 when she made the rounds leading a five-man band.

Since 1963 she has been Mrs. Jack Curtis, the wife of an industrial tool and electronics manufacturer. They have a home in Northridge, California, near Jack Oakie's,[2] and one in the Malibu colony. Her younger sister, June Hutton, who had a good career of her own as a band singer, lives in Los Angeles with her actor-husband Ken Toby.

Ina Ray Hutton had a rare combination: sexiness that turned on the men without turning away the women. Her easy disposition and manner made her welcome at anyone's party. She still gets offers from TV and nightclubs but the only job that would really tempt her would be with her beloved Los Angeles Dodgers—"Anything," she says. "I'd announce or be a cheerleader or even sell hot dogs." When the baseball season ends she spends a lot of time piloting her own plane.

Ina's famous smile is still intact.
Kermit Kelly

Mad Man with his 1952 Muntz television set. *UPI*

"MAD MAN" MUNTZ

The used-car lot king who became a household name was born Earl Muntz in Elgin, Illinois, in 1914. By the time he was ten years old he was building single-tube radio receivers, which he sold for a dollar apiece, and was wheeling and dealing among the neighborhood kids. By 1928 he had quit school and had his own business installing car radios, a rare accessory in those days.

In 1934 he bought twenty-eight old cars for $360 and opened his first used-car lot, which he later moved to Chicago. In 1941 he opened up in Los Angeles. At the suggestion of his friend Lionel Sternburger, the man who reputedly invented the cheeseburger, Muntz hired publicity man Mike Shore to make his lot at 11th Street and Figueroa the best known in town. Shore hired the artists who created Bugs Bunny to do a caricature of a man wearing long red flannels and a Napoleon hat, and "Mad Man" Muntz was born.

Jingles proclaiming Muntz the "automotive mad man" were heard on 13 radio stations 176 times a day. Skywriting and billboards informed Los Angelenos that if it weren't for his wife, the Mad Man would simply give his cars away. The message was, he bought them retail and sold them wholesale because "it's more fun that way." Not only did his huge ad budget of between $30,000 and $50,000 a month pay off handsomely but his image lent itself so easily to comedy that there was hardly a comic who didn't have at least one Mad Man Muntz joke in his routine. Jack Benny, Bob Hope, Red Skelton, and Abbott[2] & Costello made him a national joke on their radio shows. In one season alone, out of his thirty-nine programs Bob Hope made thirty-two references to Muntz, every one heard from coast to coast.

124

After the war, Earl took on the Kaiser-Frazer dealerships in New York and Los Angeles, selling $72 million worth in 1947 alone, with a personal profit (before taxes) of $1¼ million. Next came Muntz TV, a surprisingly good set with a built-in antenna and one-knob picture control. Its low price did much to bring down the cost of TV sets nationally. Working with seventy-two stores nationwide, Muntz sold $20 million by 1950. His sets were pitched as flamboyantly as were his used cars, and he even named his new baby girl Tee Vee. By then, he was also selling his Muntz Jet, an automobile that retailed for $5,500, and, at the time, the only sports car made in the United States. On this venture Muntz really lived up to his reputation: the car cost him $6,500 to manufacture. His Jet business collapsed when he was forced out of the TV company during the 1953–54 recession. But the car is still rated by the automotive experts as one of the best of its kind ever assembled domestically.

After a hiatus that lasted until 1958, Muntz was back in Hollywood with a big promotion campaign for Muntz Stereo, the first company to offer stereo tape decks for cars, including a four-track cartridge. In 1960, Muntz Stereo grossed over $30 million. Earl has since sold his interest and is back to a lot, in Van Nuys, but this time selling and renting what he feels is the big thing for the future—mobile homes.

He lives less than a mile from the lot in a huge white-on-white house, complete with tons of electronic equipment and a doorbell that plays one of his thirty-year-old jingles. The famous caricature is on almost everything in sight including his shirts. The jolly businessman is delighted with his microwave oven, four-channel stereo, and seventh wife—thirty years his junior.

Muntz, who has lost as well as made millions, likes to entertain people with the story of how he turned down the national dealership for the Volkswagen in 1951. "It was never just the money with me," he told a guest recently. "I only sell things I'd want myself and I only work with people I like."

On his terrace in Encino, California, today. *Jeanne Youngson*

In a scene from her movie swan song, *Deadline at Dawn* (1946).

LOLA LANE

The versatile screen actress was born Dorothy Mullican on May 21, 1909, in Macy, Indiana, and raised in Indianola, Iowa. By the age of twelve she was playing piano to accompany silent movies in the local theatre. She and her older sister Leota, who sang, spent hours imitating their favorite movie stars. The girls felt restricted by small town life and so Lola wrote to Gus Edwards, extravagantly describing their talents. The famed kiddie show producer was so impressed with her nerve that they were auditioned and became part of his vaudeville review. That led to a featured part in a *Greenwich Village Follies* to the lead opposite George Jessel in *War Song* (1928), on Broadway. A movie director caught *War Song* and she was signed by Fox for *Speakeasy* (1929), a big hit. She stayed with that studio for three and a half years, appearing in such features as *Good News* (1930) and *Hell Bound* (1931). After Fox failed to exercise her option, she free-lanced in low-budget features and even turned up in a serial, *Burn 'Em Up Barnes* (1935).

After Warner Brothers saw the superb work she had been doing on the first two weeks' shooting of *Marked Woman* (1937), she was signed for seven years. She did *Hollywood Hotel* (1939) with her two younger sisters, Rosemary and Priscilla Lane. These two, later going on to good careers on their own, had a break when they were singing one night on Fred Waring's radio program. Lola had called her boss, Jack Warner, and insisted he listen. All three appeared together in a series of features about a family of four girls, Gail Page played the fourth. Claude Rains was their father in these popular films, which included *Four Daughters* (1938), *Daughters Courageous* (1939), and *Four Mothers* (1941). Leota, who died some time ago, never made movies but instead for years parodied opera singers at the old Turnabout Theatre in Los Angeles

Some of Lola's other efforts were *Zanzibar* (1940) and *Mystery Ship* (1941). Her contract expired and she free-lanced briefly—very profitably. But after *Deadline at Dawn* (1946), she decided that the fun in making movies was gone, and she retired. She has never regretted it nor the many offers to appear on TV she has declined.

Lola's first marriage, for three years, was in the early 1930s, to Lew Ayres,[3] followed by movie director Al Hall, followed by nonprofessional Henry Clay Dunham, followed by movie writer-director Roland West. For twenty years now, she has been the wife of Robert Hanlon, an executive of an aircraft firm, who retired, says Lola, "when he realized he was spending his days manufacturing instruments to kill human beings." The couple live in a large circular home set in the hills facing the Pacific Ocean. The building, walled in and surrounded by rich foliage, was left to Lola by Roland West, who died in 1952. A café was once on the main floor. It was owned by film star Thelma Todd and Roland—who was the central figure in the inquest and stories that followed Miss Todd's mysterious death in 1935. No one was ever indicted.

Rosemary lives a few miles from Lola in Pacific Palisades, where she maintains a real estate office. Priscilla, the youngest is married to a retired contractor and lives in Derry, New Hampshire.

For an actress who usually played gun molls, crime reporters, or "the other woman," Lola is remarkably domestic. She sees little of the stars she knew well years ago. The Hanlons spend much of their time traveling, especially in Mexico, and their home is full of colorful objects, both collected and what Lola has made in ceramics and macramé. She loves to be recognized.

At home in California.

On radio during the 1930s.

NICK KENNY

Nicholas Napoleon Kenny, "the most widely understood poet in America," was born February 3, 1895, in Astoria, New York. His singer-bricklayer father had migrated from Ireland.

In April, 1911, Nick ran away from home and joined the navy. While in the service, he began writing poetry, which he sent to Arthur Brisbane, the columnist for the Hearst papers. After Nick's discharge on Armistice Day, 1918, he went to see Brisbane, and asked his advice. The writer suggested Kenny get some experience on a small newspaper and Nick landed a $20 a week job on the *Staten Island Advance*. In 1920, he moved to the *Bayonne* (New Jersey) *Times* where his boss was the ambitious young business manager Samuel I. Newhouse, who years later owned his own publishing empire.

Kenny worked for Walter Howey at the *Boston American*, during 1923, before switching to the *New York Journal*. There, on his day off from his job as a rewrite man, he began penning a radio column. The *New York Daily News* picked it up, but the *Mirror* liked it even more and on January 28, 1930, he began his association with that tabloid. It lasted until the day of its final edition, October 30, 1963. His "Nick Kenny Speaking" was a popular feature from the start, and it was later syndicated throughout the Hearst chain. His boss, William Randolph Hearst, was one of his greatest fans, and published his estimate of Nick: "Nick Kenny is the most inspired and inspiring poet living today." Kenny reported radio news and wrote of the personalities of the day, but it was his poetry that made him a house-hold word. Not unlike the works of Edgar Guest, Kenny's poems were simple, sentimental, and forever in praise of values that for many are the traditional ones on which America was founded. He wrote about dogs, patriotism, friendship, family. Middle Americans responded with letters and cards that exceeded those of the No. 2 man, the late Walter Winchell, by as much as 20,000 pieces a year. He often signed his work "The Old Sailor." Another of his titles was "The Heartbeat of New York."

Nick wrote the lyrics to over six hundred published songs. Two of his big hits of the 1930s are "Carelessly" and "Gold Mine in the Sky." The gold record he received for Pat Boone's one-million seller, "Love Letters in the Sand," hangs on the wall of his home in Sarasota, Florida.

Kenny was a frequent guest on radio programs of the period. He would read his poems in a voice that is a combination of Runyonesque and the croak he developed from smoking thirty cigars a day for many years.

Nick's poetry, dismissed decades ago as hopelessly corny, is still in print and is a particular favorite among the elderly and the sick. "The Cheer-up Club" his column founded has sent hundreds of thousands of greeting cards to those who have found themselves alone at difficult times. It is also incorporated in his thrice-weekly column in the *Sarasota Herald Tribune*. The newspaper material is all new of course, but his style, which he calls "dipping your pen in sunshine," is exactly as before.

Of the virtues many Americans recognize, thrift was never one well known to Kenny. He gave his two daughters everything money could buy. And now he and his wife, Kathryn, whom he married in 1927, live in a $30,000 house on his annual pension of $15,000. They used to buy a new Cadillac every year. The one they have now is a 1963 model. Mrs. Kenny says: "I needed those fur coats when I was young and pretty and had a place to wear them. No one ever lived any better than we did. I don't regret a damn thing." Their favorite restaurant is Howard Johnson's.

He still writes a column for the *Sarasota Herald Tribune. Cochran-Green*

In 1919 the leading lady to the superstar of the silents, Douglas Fairbanks, Sr.

EILEEN PERCY

The leading lady of silent pictures was born on August 1, 1899, in Belfast, Ireland. After the family moved to the United States, when she was very young, Eileen attended Catholic schools in New York and Brooklyn. One day while on a subway with two of her four sisters on their way to buy shoes, Eileen was approached by a man who offered her a role in a Broadway play. Mrs. Percy after some investigation gave her permission and Eileen made her debut on Broadway in 1910, in *The Bluebird,* playing a loaf of bread. The following year she was in *The Arab* and then in *Lady of the Slipper* in 1912, with Elsie Janis, one of the most popular stars of the day. Eileen made a lifelong friend of Marion Davies when they appeared together in *Stop! Look! Listen* in 1915. Through Elsie Janis, Eileen began appearing in the Ziegfeld Roof shows, where she was spotted by Douglas Fairbanks, Sr. Eileen had seen few movies and when the superstar asked her to test, she didn't understand what it meant. After a lengthy explanation, Fairbanks brought her to Los Angeles on a year's contract at $150 a week. Eileen was his leading lady in a number of pictures, including *Down to Earth* (1917) and *Wild and Woolly* (1917).

Despite her important connections, Eileen never became an important star although she made many silent films, some of which are *Beware of the Bride* (1920), *The Flirt* (1922), *Under the Rouge* (1925), and *Twelve Miles Out* (1927), with Joan Crawford and Betty Compson.[2] The only part she ever felt really good about was as the heavy, Aggie Lynch, in the Norma Talmadge starrer *Within the Law* (1923). She was ambitious, she says, but for security rather than a career. She did make up to $1,800 a week, but was more concerned with helping her family than in living lavishly or advancing herself as an actress.

Eileen made a few talkies but only when the director or the star was an old friend, and asked her to. She was in *Temptation* (1930) with Lois Weber (a Manhattanite and AFTRA officer) and *Sin of Madelon Claudet* (1931) with Helen Hayes.

Because of Eileen's lack of professional ambition, she was no threat to the stars of the day and she enjoyed great social popularity. She was invited to all the big Hollywood parties and was a frequent weekender at Hearst's palatial estate, San Simeon. When her good friend the late Constance Bennett married socialite Henri de la Falaise in 1932, Eileen was her maid of honor.

During the thirties Eileen wrote a society column for the *Los Angeles Examiner,* which was owned by her friend William Randolph Hearst. She had been divorced from her first husband, Elric Bush, five years when she met songwriter Harry Ruby at a party given by director George Fitzmaurice. They were married shortly thereafter, in 1936, when she retired.

In 1950 M-G-M filmed a musical, *Three Little Words,* based loosely on the lives of Harry Ruby and his lyricist partner, Burt Kalmar. Eileen was portrayed by Arlene Dahl.

Ruby's ample income from his movie scores and his royalties from such standards penned by him over the years as "Who's Sorry Now?" and "Nevertheless" has provided the couple with the means for the good life. Until Eileen's two recent heart attacks they gave parties, played golf, and traveled extensively. During the last few years, however, her activities have been card games and visits with old friends like Evelyn Brent[3] and Viola Dana (working in a dress shop and living in Santa Monica) .

As Mrs. Harry Ruby in Beverly Hills where she lives a very quiet life. *Jeannie Phillips*

Captain Video warns his Video Ranger of danger in the distance in 1950.

CAPTAIN VIDEO: Al Hodge

In 1949 the Du Mont Television Network produced the first and most successful space series, "Captain Video," with Richard Coogan in the title role. The original concept of the interplanetary adventurer was to host western films in the late afternoon for school children. The success of the program, however, was immediate, and it went from fifteen minutes each day, Monday through Friday, to thirty minutes. Du Mont also began talking about merchandising Captain Video helmets and games, but when Coogan asked for a piece of the action the network replaced him with Al Hodge. Hodge, who took over the character after it had been on the air six months, previously starred on radio for eight years as the Green Hornet and had directed such shows as "Challenge of the Yukon" and "The Lone Ranger."

Captain Video's one and only Video Ranger was Don Hastings, who was fifteen years old when he got the part. Hastings and Hodge, who were on five days a week, mixed it up with such regulars as Tony Randall, Jack Klugman, Arnold Stang, and the late Ruth White. Probably the best remembered was Ernest Borgnine, who got his first acting break with the part of Nargola. Captain Video, who asked and gave no quarter, was in constant peril from such heavies as Prince Komar of the "festering black planet," but the arch villain who seemed to be behind all dastardly plots was the sinister Dr. Pauley played to a fare-thee-well by Hal Conklin. So seriously did the kids who lived near Conklin in Levittown, Long Island, take his unpleasant deeds that on several occasions they broke his windows and once tore up his entire front lawn.

The show at the beginning emanated from the now-gone Wanamaker's department store at 12th Street and Broadway in Manhattan, with an all-novice production staff and technical crew. "Everyone worked with everyone else," comments Hodge. "No one did just one thing. I've never seen such teamwork before or since in this business." Everything was done as inexpensively as possible. Only in the last couple of years were the actors' tacky uniforms replaced with decently fitting ones. The prop budget must have set some kind of a record with a weekly maximum expenditure of five dollars.

For most of the time "Captain Video" was sponsored by Powerhouse Candy Bars. At the commercials a huge cardboard candy bar was pulled apart to show the kids what wonderful things it contained. "The trouble was, with lighting and reception being what it was, it looked like two large sewer entrances," says Hodge of the cardboard bar.

When the series went off the air on April 1, 1955, Hodge was put to work hosting a kiddie-cartoon show for the remaining year of his contract. To the end, it was the top-rated children's program on the air but plans to resume it as a syndicated show and of a revival by NBC came to nothing. Since Du Mont folded shortly afterward, no care was taken to preserve publicity stills, scripts, or kinescopes of the shows and the few that exist are in the libraries of universities and in private hands.

Don Hastings is constantly reminded by fellow actors of the "equations of doom," and "torpedo lances," and his constant cry of "Holy Hyperion!" Don has been a regular on TV soap operas such as "As the World Turns" and "Edge of Night" following his years as the Video Ranger.

Al Hodge, however, was so typecast by his role that he has since been forced to work for a temporary employment service. Both actors during the show's run made much more in personal appearance fees than they did in salaries from Du Mont. Hodge, recently leaving his Manhattan apartment to dub a commercial, was stopped by a stranger in his late twenties who asked if Hodge was going to his "secret mountain headquarters on the planet earth, to rally men of good will and lead them against the forces of evil everywhere." Said Al: "I'm glad he didn't offer to follow me as I rocket from planet to planet defending justice, truth, and freedom throughout the universe."

Reunited for an interview at WBAI-FM studios in New York. *Peter Schaeffer*

As a single after he got out of the army.

BOB EBERLY

The bobby-soxers' idol of the big band era was born the first of eight children on July 24, 1916, in Mechanicville, New York, and brought up in nearby Hoosick Falls.

He had sung only a little, locally, when he won a 1935 amateur contest on Fred Allen's radio program. The prize was $50 plus another $50 in salary for a week's engagement at New York's Roxy Theatre. Later that year he was hired for a night to sing with the Dorsey Brothers in Troy, New York. Dorsey's vocalist, Bob Crosby, had just left them. The professional association endured nine years, and a friendship with Jimmy Dorsey, who soon took over the group, lasted until Jimmy's death on June 12, 1957. Bob was so well liked among the musicians that neither the audience hysteria he created nor his romance with the band's pretty songstress, Helen O'Connell,[3] ever caused any resentment. Even at the height of his fame, when fans tore his clothes to shreds and screamed until he couldn't even hear the music, he never lost his temper or his famous sense of humor.

He was much better looking than Frank Sinatra and Bob never had to hire claques to swoon at his performances. Sinatra's anxiety to get out of his contract with Tommy Dorsey, Sinatra admits, stemmed from his fear that if Eberly had gone out as a single first, Sinatra would never have been able to make it as big as he did. Bob, who never had a contract with Jimmy Dorsey, could have left any time. However, the most he ever made at that job was $400 a week, plus another $1,250 while making a picture. But Bob wasn't ambitious and he "never felt adequate," even though people like Dick Haymes,[2] after becoming a big star, admitted that Eberly was his idol. The lucrative offers to promote him as a single or build a big band around him never excited him. Paramount Pictures felt they could make him into a big star but the only movies Bob made were with the Dorsey aggregation: *The Fleet's In* (1942), *I Dood It* (1943), and *The Fabulous Dorseys* (1947).

After being drafted in December, 1943, he spent two years in Special Services, most of it as vocalist for the Wayne King orchestra then entertaining GIs. On discharge, despite a diminished popularity, Bob found working as a single far more profitable than before. He was considered for radio's "Chesterfield Supper Club" but Perry Como got the job.

Bob has been married since January 28, 1940, to Florine Callahan, a former Ziegfeld Girl. They live in Great Neck, Long Island, with their large family. Son Bob is a singer. Bob's brother Ray, who lives in Lake Park, Florida, works now and then with Tex Beneke. Brother Walter, who had a short career as a singer, is with the Rockwell Tool Company in Mississippi.

Bob continues to sing in clubs, and his career is very much on the upswing now. He sings mostly with Lee Castle and the Jimmy Dorsey Band and occasionally with Vaughn Monroe. For the bigger dates, Castle flies in Helen O'Connell from Los Angeles and the two are reunited singing their smash hits of the late thirties and early forties: "Green Eyes," "Amapola," "Tangerine," "Deep Purple," and "I Remember You."

With musicologist George Simon (*left*) at WBAI-FM studios in New York. *Michael Knowles*

From his 1942 film, *This Was Paris,* made in England.

BEN LYON

The leading man of the screen was born on February 6, 1901, in Atlanta, Georgia. His father was a successful businessman and his mother, who was born in Germany, was renowned locally as a great beauty. When Ben was four years old, the family moved to Baltimore, where he eventually attended the exclusive Park School. In 1916, he arrived in New York City, where he was enrolled in a prep school. But he soon fell in love with the movie industry, which had not yet moved its center to Hollywood. One of his close friends at the time was a pretty and ambitious hatcheck girl named Norma Shearer.[1]

Against his better judgment, Ben's father subsidized him while the teenager sought out work as an extra, which paid $3 a day. After touring the country for two seasons, beginning in 1918, with *Seventeen,* Ben supported the legendary Jeanne Eagels in her play *The Wonderful Thing* (1920). He had small parts in such pictures as *Open Your Eyes* (1919) and *The Heart of Maryland* (1921), but he longed to be a star. Sam Goldwyn saw him in the play *Mary The Third* and signed him for his film *Potash and Perlmutter* (1923). Then he got *Flaming Youth* (1923), which starred Colleen Moore,[2] and a five-year contract with First National.

Ben worked steadily through the silent era, appearing with a dazzling array of female stars—Gloria Swanson, Anna Q. Nilsson,[3] Blanche Sweet,[1] Barbara La Marr, Pauline Starke (living in Santa Monica), and Pola Negri, who, for some reason unknown to Ben, disliked him. His credits during the era include *So Big* (1925), *The Savage* (1926), *The Tender Hour* (1927), and *For the Love of Mike* (1927), with Claudette Colbert.

When sound came to Hollywood he continued to remain active, doing *The Flying Marine* (1929), with Shirley Mason (the widow of director Sidney Lanfield and living in Palm Springs; Shirley's sister, Viola Dana, works in a dress shop in Westwood Village, California), *Indiscreet* (1931),

Hat Check Girl (1932), *I Cover the Waterfront* (1933), and *Frisco Water-front* (1935), with the late Helen Twelvetrees.

If Ben Lyon rates as a movie immortal it would be for his part in the classic *Hell's Angels* (1930). Although it was never released, the silent version starred Ben and Greta Nissen; it was decided that her accent was too heavy for the sound version and Lyon suggested Jean Harlow, then almost an unknown, as a replacement. During the filming, he and the other players played jokes on the young producer, Howard Hughes. Ben regrets them today: "We used to pretend we were talking about him when we were actually only moving our lips. Even then his hearing was very poor. He took it very well, but it really wasn't funny when I look back on it. I never think about it that I don't feel ashamed."

In 1936, Ben and his wife, the late Bebe Daniels,[1] left Hollywood to accept an offer from London's Palladium. They also thought they would avoid kidnap threats, so common at the time in the movie colony. They were just as popular in the British Isles, doing vaudeville tours, feature films, and several highly successful radio and TV series.

For a number of years Ben was director of casting for Twentieth Century-Fox in England and is credited with bringing Marilyn Monroe to the studio. However, whenever the subject comes up he is quick to add that he also turned down Leslie Caron ("Truthfully, I couldn't see a thing to her—then!") and Audrey Hepburn because Audrey took too long to answer a note he had sent backstage.

After he left Fox, Ben headed his own talent agency in London, but gave that up after his wife Bebe Daniels died in 1970. A year later he married his costar from the silent days, the widow of director William Seiter, Marion Nixon. After a long honeymoon on the Continent, the couple moved to an apartment on Wilshire Boulevard in Westwood, California.

Marion and Ben on their return from a recent vacation. *Antoinette Lopopolo*

With the former Mrs. John F. Kennedy, then the wife of the Senator, at the April in Paris ball, 1954. *UPI*

SLOAN SIMPSON

The former First Lady of New York City was born Elizabeth Sloan Simpson in Dallas, Texas, in 1917, to post middle-age parents. Her mother was a Baltimore debutante and her father a friend of Teddy Roosevelt's. He had served as a GOP postmaster, contracted TB, and lost all his money when Sloan was very young. But he managed to send their only child to an exclusive convent school in Pennsylvania.

Sloan began to be known publicly when she embarked on a career in acting and modeling. That followed her divorce, in 1943, from her five-year marriage to attorney Carroll Dewey Hipp. Although she did extremely well in her work, she never liked herself in photographs.

When Sloan met William O'Dwyer at the celebration of New York City's Golden Anniversary party in 1949, she was one of the top models and fashion consultants in the country. And O'Dwyer had just been elected to his second term as mayor. On December 20 of that year, they were married in Florida in a Roman Catholic ceremony (O'Dwyer was a widower and Sloan's first marriage had not been before a priest).

In the one year she reigned at Gracie Mansion Sloan made quite a splash. *Life* put her on its cover and she seemed to be everywhere at once. Although she says she would never have sought a public life, she relished much of what it brought her, and was a great favorite among newspaper people, particularly with photographers. However, she resented the emphasis on "appearances." Once when she ordered a dinner of pheasant for a visiting VIP, she was told that steak had to be substituted. When she argued that filet mignon was even more expensive, the mayor explained that that was not exactly the point. How would it look to the public?

In 1950 Mayor O'Dwyer resigned his office to become President Truman's Ambassador to Mexico. But everyone knew that the reformer, elected in 1945 (by the highest margin ever given a mayoralty candidate), was leaving more to get away from the exposure of political corruption in the O'Dwyer Administration bared by Senator Kefauver's committee hearings. Although he was never charged with direct involvement in the scandals, he left for Mexico City, his once promising political career ruined.

When O'Dwyer resigned his ambassadorial post a year later, his marriage was in even worse shape than his finances. They got a Mexican divorce in 1953 and Sloan received a small settlement. The two remained good friends until he died in November 1964.

During the 1950s, "the second Mrs. Simpson," as she was dubbed to distinguish her from the Duchess of Windsor, had a fling at acting on the strawhat circuit, in what she refers to as "roles for the poor man's Celeste Holm." And she spent two seasons on WOR and ABC television and radio in New York City hostessing her own talk shows. Her one film, *The Pusher* (1960), was not a success.

Since 1957, Sloan has been in Acapulco, where she opened a travel advisory bureau. She is now salaried by Braniff Airlines and provides for anyone who cares to call her—anything from a baby-sitter to a Rolls-Royce (with chauffeur). Listed in the telephone book as Sloan, she is the person to see in the resort town if one wants to give a party for the "in" crowd.

A registered Republican when she married Democrat O'Dwyer, Sloan says she now votes for the man rather than the party. She is a United States citizen with legal residence in Mexico.

Very much in the social swim in Acapulco. *Antoinette Lopopolo*

In his 1934 talkie *The Trail Drive*—matters in hand, as usual.

KEN MAYNARD

The sagebrush hero of silent and sound films was born on July 21, 1885, in Vevey, Indiana. At the age of eighteen, had had mastered the trick riding that was to dazzle millions at the famous King Ranch, before joining the Buffalo Bill Wild West Show. In 1913, the show folded and he spent the next six years with the Ringling Brothers Wild West Show. In 1920, promoter Tex Rickard put Ken into rodeo competition. In his first time out he walked off with the title of "World's Champion Cowboy" and a $42,000 prize.

While performing his stunts with a show in Los Angeles, a friend took him for his first tour of a movie studio. Lynn Reynolds, one of Tom Mix's directors, asked him how he would like to do some of his extraordinary riding in a movie, and he made his debut playing Paul Revere in *Judith Meredith* (1924). Tiffany Studios put him under contract at a salary Ken thought to be easy money—until he discovered that the producers expected him to star in two productions simultaneously. Ken shuttled between sets with a different horse, cast, and script, a common practice for many years among B producers.

The Ken Maynard features remembered so fondly by silent western fans were those made from 1926 on, after Ken moved to First National. Here the production pace slackened somewhat and the quality of the product improved greatly. From here, the image of the big, handsome guy with the white hat was projected throughout the world. Immaculately groomed and rather flashily dressed, Ken appeared in such "oaters" as *Wild Horse Stampede* (1926) and *The Red Raiders* (1927). He put his famous horse, Tarzan, through paces unmatched by any other western star.

Talking pictures proved a fine medium for him, as he sounded **exactly** like what he was—a cowboy. And contrary to general belief, although Ken never had more than an adequate voice, he and not Gene Autry introduced song to the western movie. A few of his talkies were *Lucky Larkin* (1930), *Dynamite Ranch* (1932), *Fargo Express* (1933), *In Old Santa Fe* (1934), with Evalyn Knapp (the widow of a physician and living in West Hollywood, California) and *Avenging Waters* (1936).

Ken left the movies in 1938 and toured the rodeo circuits for five years. When he returned it was to costar with his old pal Hoot Gibson and the younger Bob Steele in a series of Monogram cheapies. After 1945 he returned to personal appearances at fairs and rodeos, where he continued to draw audiences until he was well into his fifties.

Maynard never made the kind of money due a star of his stature. He had his big chance in the thirties, when he had his own production unit, but his lack of discipline and his refusal to take direction was reflected on the screen—and at the box office. "Nobody could tell Ken anything. He knew it all." That's the comment of a Hollywood veteran from many a Maynard film. Another problem, which continues to this day, was alcohol, which caused his drinking buddy, W. C. Fields, to chide him about the hypocrisy of his upright screen image.

The man who for several years was among the top screen money-makers lives alone in a ramshackle trailer filled with dusty mementos of his years of glory. His wife, the former circus aerialist Bertha Denham, died in 1969, and his brother Kermit Maynard, who had a good career of his own as a western star, died in 1970. He consented to appear on a network TV show "for the money," but had appeared to be so drunk by taping time that the host could not interview him. However, his behavior on the program, which was not cut, was quite noticeable when he shouted remarks during the interviews with several other stars of silent days.

In his trailer in San Fernando, California. *Michael Knowles*

In 1946, on the "Hour of Charm" on radio in the late afternoon on Sunday. *CBS*

EVELYN AND HER MAGIC VIOLIN

The musical star of radio was born Evelyn Kaye Klein in New York City's "Little Hungary." Her family was poor but enthusiastic about her interest in music. And somehow money was found to give her violin lessons. At thirteen, Evelyn won a gold medal and then, while a student at Juilliard, she was awarded a scholarship to the Damrosch Institute, she won the Fontainebleau Grand Prix, in France, and took the MacDowell Club Award and the National Arts Club Competition.

One evening, in the depths of the Depression, Phil Spitalny[1] heard Evelyn's debut at Town Hall. That convinced him of the soundness of his long-held idea for an all-girl orchestra. When he went to see her the next day, her grandmother slammed the door in his face. She thought he was "a dirty old man." Undaunted, Spitalny slid a note under the door, asking the teen-ager to audition. He also enclosed a pair of tickets to the Capitol Theatre, where he was then appearing. Evelyn came with her mother, and she was signed to an exclusive contract. Spitalny then auditioned over one thousand girls, twenty-seven of whom he hired.

Their debut was at the Capitol Theatre in 1934. By the time they reached radio in January, 1935, Evelyn, now the concertmaster and featured soloist, had named the show "The Hour of Charm." It ran almost two decades on network radio, with the sponsorship of General Electric. On radio and in their many tours of presentation houses, Evelyn was featured front and center. Her billing, "Evelyn and Her Magic Violin," which Spitalny gave her early in their association, was advertised as prominently as his.

The aggregation was remarkable in that they got along so well, they were never touched by scandal, and they played consistently fine music from a repertory limited to light opera and melodic pop tunes. Their discipline and spirit always was attributed to Evelyn, the group spokeswoman and authority figure.

Evelyn is a strong advocate of women's rights. "To be a musician a woman has to be a fine one. We have to be better than men just to be taken seriously, and then one sour note, which any male is permitted, and we get that 'just like a woman' routine." Spitalny, her husband since 1946, concurred, adding that he knew of nothing a man could do in music that a woman couldn't, "except maybe move a grand piano."

The Spitalnys retired in 1955 and wrote music reviews for a newspaper in Miami. "We became good listeners," says Evelyn, the music editor for the *Miami Beach Reporter*. She also writes the program notes for the Miami Philharmonic. Evelyn has established the Evelyn and Phil Spitalny scholarships at the University of Miami for female violinists and male conductors. Her husband died in 1970 and she now tours Europe each summer, covering the music festivals for her paper. After Phil died she vowed never to play her Bergonzi, but she missed her music, if not the applause. She practices daily in a soundproof studio behind her house. Her two great friends are Harry Brandt's widow (Harry was the theatre magnate who used to terrify Hollywood stars each year when he released his dreaded "Box Office Poison" list) and Vivian Shaw, sister of Robert Shaw. Vivian was a featured vocalist of "The Hour of Charm," billed as the "Golden Voice of Vivian." (Mrs. Brandt lives near Evelyn in Miami and Vivian is married to a prominent Beverly Hills surgeon, Dr. Frederick Schlumberger.)

In the doorway of her Miami Beach
home today. *Kendra Kerr*

A 1940 publicity still from Universal Pictures.

EDDIE QUILLAN

The googly-eyed comedian and character actor was born in Philadelphia on March 31, 1907. By the time he was seven years old Eddie was performing in vaudeville with his sister and three brothers in an act called "The Rising Generation." The Quillan kids did well on stage but they loved the movies and begged their father-manager to get them work in motion pictures. The elder Quillan knew Nick Harris of the famous detective agency. Harris happened to know Mack Sennett. When the kids were in Los Angeles, booked at the Orpheum Theatre in 1925, they approached the producer and were given a screen test. It was run a few days later, but it so discouraged them that they walked out of the projection room before it was over. Sennett, however, was very impressed, but only with Eddie, who he signed to a contract.

Quillan made eighteen two-reelers, beginning with *A Love Sundae* (1926). But he balked at doing a blue bit in one of the scripts and walked off the lot forever. He free-lanced for a while, getting good parts in such silent features as *Show Folks* (1928). Cecil B. de Mille offered him a small role in *The Godless Girl* (1929) but he turned it down. It impressed the director so much he gave Eddie the comedy lead. After that he played the lead in Leo McCarey's first feature, *The Sophomore* (1929).

Eddie's double-take, which he developed on the stage and mastered in silents, combined with his youthful enthusiasm, got him lots of work in talkies. He thinks his best was *Big Money* (1930). His other credits include *Girl Crazy* (1932), *Strictly Personal* (1933), *Mutiny on the Bounty* (1935),

Big City (1937), *Young Mr. Lincoln* (1939), with Marjorie Weaver (owner of a liquor store in Brentwood, California), *Grapes of Wrath* (1940), and *The Kid Glove Killer* (1942). In *Mutiny* and *Grapes* he was surrounded by some of the top talent in Hollywood. In his small parts in them he turned in performances so natural and touching he was singled out for praise by critics and fellow actors. But producers continued to cast him as a bellhop, an elevator man, and a soda jerk. Although he worked constantly, it was in B pictures like *It Ain't Hay* (1943) and *This Is the Life* (1944).

In the mid-forties Eddie tried his luck at owning a bowling alley in nearby El Monte. But when *Brigadoon* (1954) came along he was glad to be back in the picture business.

A few years ago he sold the big house he had bought during his peak years. He now lives with his two unmarried sisters in a smaller one in North Hollywood. Their youngest brother, the late Joe Quillan, penned many shows on radio and TV for Eddie Cantor and Joan Davis as well as nearly all the "Our Miss Brooks" series. The Quillans are devout Roman Catholics and religious objects are displayed throughout the house; a large statue of the Blessed Virgin rests in the backyard.

Never really a part of the Hollywood social scene, Quillan, who has never married, has one close friend in the profession: Lloyd Nolan.

Although the past two decades haven't been so good, Eddie has always managed to make a living on TV and in movies. Producer Hal Kantor, one of his greatest fans, found a lot of work for him on the recent "Julia" series. "You need someone up top looking out for you," says Eddie. "Casting directors are so young these days they haven't a clue as to who I am or what I've done. How do you tell someone you've been in over one hundred movies?"

Enjoying a joke in the yard of his San Fernando Valley home. *Stephen Radich*

Most of Big Sister's troubles were far more serious than the one in this 1947 publicity still.

"BIG SISTER"

On September 14, 1936, the town hall clock in Glens Falls tolled for the first time and one of the most abused characters in all radio soap operadom was heard throughout North America.

Fictional Ruth Evans Wayne and her husband, Dr. John Wayne, lived in this community surrounded by friends, family, and trouble. The character of big-sister-wife-mother was written by Lillian Lauferty and was owned and coauthored by Julian Funt, who had a co-writer, Bob Newman. The program was known for many years as "Rinso's Big Sister" and was greatly responsible for promoting the Lever Brothers' "Rinso white" jingle. At one point, Funt pulled off a deal that is still unique in broadcasting. He took the series away from Lever, the original sponsor, and sold it to their arch rival, Proctor and Gamble, for more money.

Five days a week "Big Sister" held forth on CBS Radio in the early afternoons, delaying shopping and housework in millions of homes. It was so popular that one of its early lead characters, Michael West, was spun off into another soap, "Bright Horizon," with Big Sister at first appearing on that program until it was able to hold its own.

When the "Big Sister" show debuted, Ruth was unmarried—until it was discovered single heroines were of little interest to housewives who identified only with their own.

Once Ruth became Mrs. John Wayne she was spared nothing in the way of marital misery. Her husband was for quite a while interned in a Japanese prisoner-of-war camp. And not only were there other women in his life, but one, Hope, turned out to be the wife of Neddie, Ruth's younger brother.

Ruth, of course, would never dream of cheating on John although John's best friend, Reed Bannister, played by Barry Kroger, was obviously in love with Ruth, and had been for years. Being the noble souls they were, Ruth and Reed never came out and discussed it but a loyal listener knew that they really both "knew in their hearts."

There was also Ruth's seemingly ageless little boy, originally played by Jim Ameche's son and then by a woman. But the biggest thorn in Ruth's side was Neddie, who, instead of completing school and getting his Ph.D., as she had planned, became a garage mechanic and married the rather disagreeable Hope. A younger sister, Sue Evans, was originally played by Dorothy McGuire.

The first Big Sister was Alice Frost (still active in Los Angeles TV), who was replaced by Nancy Marshall. The late Margie Anderson was third, with Mercedes McCambridge taking over for a time before Grace Matthews stepped in during 1946. Grace played it through the last broadcast—with Richard Leibert, as usual, at the organ playing "Valse Bluette"—which was the day after Christmas, 1952. Grace is very active in television and is often kept so late at the studios that she is unable to get a train back to the home she shares in Chappaqua, New York, with husband, actor Court Benson.

Recently Grace Matthews laughingly remarked that her former faithful listeners might like to know that she sees Ruth and Dr. John, still together, often, through the courtesy of Paul McGrath and his wife, when she stays over in their Park Avenue apartment in New York. McGrath, who played the small-town doctor for many years, often refers to his fictional self as "the idiot husband" because of Dr. John's many bouts with amnesia.

Grace Matthews with Paul McGrath in a visit to his Manhattan apartment. *Michael Knowles*

Paramount's "Rock of Gibraltar" in 1930.

CLIVE BROOK

The stalwart leading man of motion pictures was born Clifford Brook in London on June 1, 1886. His mother, Charlotte Mary Brook, the opera singer, and his father wanted Clive to study law. They were able to send him to outstanding private schools, until 1901 when they suffered financial reverses. Clive gave up plans to become a barrister when he left Dulwich College at the age of 15. He then studied elocution at Polytechnic, where he did so well he became a teacher. After graduation he put in a stint as the assistant secretary of the Colonial Club in London before working for a while as a newspaper reporter. He also had some success at the time writing and selling short stories before entering the British Army, September, 1914, as a private. When he left the service at the end of World War I, a major, he decided to pursue the career he had really always wanted, which was nourished at fourteen years of age, when he had first acted.

Brook began making silent films in England and was seen in *Debt of Honor* (1918) as well as some plays. He married his costar Mildred Evelyn from the play *Fair and Warmer* when they appeared in it in 1920. He made *The Royal Oak* (1920), with Betty Compson,[2] and as soon as it was shown in Hollywood he was offered contracts with three studios. He first went with Thomas Ince and then to Warner Brothers for a short time. The period for which he is remembered best came during his eight years with Paramount, beginning in 1926. Although he complained continually that he was weary of playing only cads or terribly correct gentlemen, the studio continued to cast him in those roles. Adolph Zukor once told him that he always thought of Brook as the "Rock of Gibraltar."

Some of Clive Brook's better work was done in *Woman to Woman* (1924), *Three Faces East* (1926) with Jetta Goudal (the wife of interior decorator Howard Grieve and living in Los Angeles), *Underworld* (1927), *Four Feathers* (1929), *The Return of Sherlock Holmes* (1929), *Slightly Scarlet* (1930), *Shanghai Express* (1932), and *Cavalcade* (1933).

There was never any question that Clive Brook would survive the advent of sound. His precise speech made him more sought after than ever. With his old friend William Powell[2] and Evelyn Brent[3] he appeared in Paramount's first all-talkie, *Interference* (1928). When his Paramount contract expired he went to R-K-O, but by 1936 partly because he and his wife were beside themselves over the threats to kidnap their children, they moved permanently to England. At this time the entire movie colony was alarmed as kidnapping incidents and attempts grew. For a while Brook slept with a revolver under his pillow and his children, a boy and a girl, were taken to school each day by a private policeman their family shared with Ann Harding (retired in Westport, Connecticut).

Brook had always wanted to return to the stage. In England he made more films such as *The Ware Case* (1939) and *Convoy* (1941), but most of his efforts were in the theatre. He both acted and directed quite successfully. The movie *On Approval* (1945), which he produced, directed, and acted in with Bea Lillie (living on Manhattan's East End Avenue), was a huge hit and is considered by Clive to be his best. Occasionally he watches some of the talkies he made with stars such as Ruth Chatterton and Tallulah Bankhead but feels he was "stiff and perfectly awful" in them.

He has appeared in a number of plays on the BBC and is very proud of his daughter Faith's success as an actress. Although he doesn't consider himself retired, he has not made a movie since *The List of Adrian Messenger* (1963).

Brook, who is currently working on his autobiography, and his wife live in a large, luxuriously furnished flat on Eaton Square, directly across from Elisabeth Bergner's.[1] The Brooks usually spend their winters in the Bahamas, and in spite of his age, Brook swims almost daily. He is very active socially; occasionally he runs into Marlene Dietrich, whom he knew very well during his days at Paramount when he and the late Josef von Sternberg were close. Says Brook: "She was always such a beautiful, simple girl then. She used to cook delicious food and bring it to us each morning on the set. Now she's like a character from one of her films. Seems to be playing Marlene Dietrich."

Enjoying his retirement in the Caribbean sun. *Kirk Crivello*

She brought her famous expensive look to movies in 1930.

GENEVIEVE TOBIN

The petite star of stage and screen was born around 1905 on 34th Street in New York City. Her mother, a tiny woman with a formidable personality, was known in theatrical circles as "Little Tobin," and generally ran the professional and private lives of her two daughters Genevieve and Vivian. Vivian, who became a name on Broadway and in movies, married a doctor and retired to Montecito, California, after her appearance in Cecil B. De Mille's *Sign of the Cross* (1932). The lack of money in the family instilled ambition in all three women.

Genevieve left P.S. 54 to take a part in *Palmy Days* (1919). The play, which was directed by Monty Woolley, was a hit and she never went back to school. The next year she had another success in *Little Old New York,* which she followed with Guy Bolton's *Polly Preferred* (1923). Leslie Howard chose her to costar with him in the play he wrote, *Murray Hill* (1927).

By this time, she was very much the Broadway star and offstage lived the kind of glamorous life often pictured in movies but seldom experienced even by celebrities. Her escorts were society's most eligible bachelors, among them Laddie Sanford and Joseph O'Donohue IV (working on his memoirs in San Francisco). Genevieve was very beautiful, slightly aloof, and had a reputation for being both a lot of fun and well behaved at the same time.

On November 27, 1929, with the country still reeling from the Great Crash of a few weeks before, she opened on Broadway in *50 Million Frenchmen*. In it, Genevieve and William Gaxton introduced "You Do Something to Me." Until then, its author, Cole Porter, had had nothing but flops, but when the final curtain fell, he and his cast were the toasts of New York.

Genevieve turned down an M-G-M contract resulting from her role in Universal's *A Lady Surrenders* (1930); she proved to be as delightful at high comedy in films as she had been on stage. She did some delicious work in the Chevalier-MacDonald starrer, *One Hour With You* (1932), and then went to London to make *Perfect Understanding* (1933) with Gloria Swanson. She was also in *Broadway Hostess* (1935), with Lyle Talbot (living in Los Angeles), *The Petrified Forest* (1936), *The Great Gambini* (1937), with the late Akim Tamiroff, *Yes, My Darling Daughter* (1939), with Priscilla Lane (Mrs. Joseph A. Howard of Derry, New Hampshire), and Jeffrey Lynn (a real estate dealer in the San Fernando Valley with seven children), and *Queen of Crime* (1941), with Googie Withers (living in Australia).

On September 20, 1938, Genevieve married a prominent film and theatre director, William Keighley, who discouraged her from working. She wanted very much to appear on the "Lux Radio Theatre," which he hosted from 1945 to 1955, but she was never asked. To this day she has never asked him why she was not invited.

During World War II, Genevieve lived in Washington, where Keighley made films for the government.

When Keighley retired from motion-picture making in the mid-fifties, the couple moved to Paris, where they live in a large, luxurious, ultramodern apartment on the fashionable Avenue Foch. Until Keighley's stroke in 1972, they traveled constantly, and are still very much part of the Parisian social scene. One of their close friends is Guy Bolton.

Genevieve has lost none of the chic and vivacity that once made her a favorite of cafe society. When asked recently if she regretted retiring so early, she replied: "When you're a poor Irish girl and people tell you how pretty you are, you go on the stage. My career was a very exciting means to a very happy end. It gave me wonderful friends, money, and a very good marriage. It lasted just long enough."

Genevieve and William Keighley on the terrace of their Paris flat. *Don Koll*

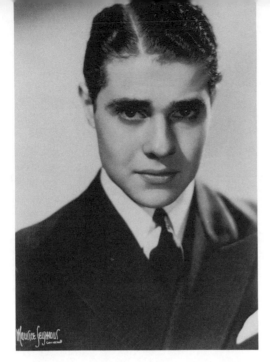

The young Jim Ameche as Jack Armstrong, the All-American Boy.

JACK ARMSTRONG: Jim Ameche

The adventure serial that kept young Americans glued to their radios for nearly two decades began at station WBBM in Chicago on July 31, 1933. Jim Ameche, then a recent arrival from Kenosha, Wisconsin, took on the title role, while his older brother, Don, played the part of Captain Hughes. Don left the show after only a few months when it was decided that the brothers' voices were too similar, and of course became a famous movie star. Jim stayed with the series through early 1939 when he left for Hollywood.

The sponsor, Wheaties (referred to on the air as the Breakfast of Champions), bought time for the program on all of CBS's 90-odd stations but added about twenty independents as well, which meant that the show had to be transcribed. Recording of radio programs was very rare in those days, and the means were primitive by today's standards. Three weeks before each broadcast, the cast, gathered around a microphone in a studio atop the Chicago Daily News Building, and performed each script until they had one absolutely perfect recording on the huge wax discs. Editing was impossible.

A group called The Norsemen sang the famous theme that began: "Wave the flag for Hudson High [Jack's school], boys. Show them how we stand!"

Other characters were Billy Fairfield (for a time played by TV star Dick York) and his sister Betty and their Uncle Jim, the show's father figure, played for the run of the program by James Goss. Uncle Jim owned an aircraft factory and took them all on adventures in his hydroplane, *The Silver Albatross,* or in a dirigible or an autogiro.

Robert Hardy Andrews, who created and wrote the serial, fashioned a latter-day Frank Merriwell that a naive generation could identify with. The character's consistent uprightness today would be laughable but the All-American Boy was taken very seriously by his listeners and sponsors. The program's first giveaway (in return for the cereal box tops) in its first year on the air moved Wheaties off every North American grocery shelf within days. General Mills still hasn't found a program that could sell their product the way "Jack Armstrong" did. Probably few remember the fifteen-minute episodes better than the Depression kids who couldn't raise the 10 or 15 cents that had to be included with the Wheaties box top for a Jack Armstrong hike-o-meter, Torpedo Flashlite, whistling ring, or Norden bombsight. Announcer Franklyn MacCormack put it to listeners in none-too-subtle terms during the 1940s that boys and girls who were not eating Wheaties simply weren't doing their bit for the war effort.

The second Jack Armstrong was St. John Terrell in 1939, and he was replaced by Stanley Harris and then by Rye Billsbury. When it went off the air in 1951 Charles Flynn had the lead, and the series had moved from CBS to NBC and finally to ABC. During most of its years it was heard at 5:30 P.M. Mondays through Fridays. By the time of its demise Uncle Jim had stepped aside for a younger character, Vic Hardy, who headed the Scientific Bureau of Investigation (the SBI) in which Jack, Billy, and Betty were enrolled. During its 1951 run ABC tried the characters on a thrice-weekly thirty-minute show called "Armstrong of the SBI" but it never caught on.

Jim Ameche, who claimed for "Jack Armstrong" the best training ground a radio performer could hope for despite the low pay and long hours in non-air-conditioned studios, is still active as an announcer and moderator in radio and television. He lives in Beverly Hills with his wife Mary.

To no one's surprise "Jack Armstrong" was never attempted on television. By the time it went off radio, America had grown up.

Outside his Los Angeles home. *Jerry Beirne*

Flanked by Ron Morris, who placed second, and E. Landstroem of Finland, who was third, in his moment of triumph. *UPI*

DON BRAGG

The pole vaulter who won the gold medal for the United States in the 1960 Olympics was born in a poor, racially mixed neighborhood in Penns Grove, New Jersey, on May 5, 1935. As a young boy he was slender and introverted, with a serious inferiority complex. But he began to change in physique and personality after getting recognition in sports. He won scholarships in basketball and football but concentrated on pole vaulting when it became obvious that he did that best.

By the time he enrolled at Villanova, Don had already decided on his life's goal—to be the world's champion pole vaulter. At the Olympic tryouts in 1956 he was eliminated because of a technicality. But this only strengthened his determination and he dedicated himself totally for the next four years.

His Olympic win in Rome in the summer of 1960 proved to Don what he had felt for years—he was the best pole vaulter in the world. He had bettered by one inch the previous world's record of 15 feet set in 1933 by Cornelius Warmerdam, the Flying Dutchman (now the athletic coach at Fresno State College in California).

In interview after interview the new Olympic star expressed his intention to play Tarzan on the screen, and spent a year waiting around Hollywood for a promised production to begin. He even turned down a part in *The*

Chapman Report. When his chance to play the jungle hero came, he cut his foot and the producer was unwilling to wait six weeks. The third and last time in the movies he actually completed three-fourths of a feature, in Jamaica, when a legal dispute impounded the film. It has never been completed or seen. These were great disappointments to Don but nothing compared to what he would have felt had he failed in Rome: "I'd have killed myself," he says. But he has always thought of himself as Tarzan and still signs autographs Don Tarzan Bragg.

Bragg believes anything would have been anticlimactic after his Olympic triumph, and for the last seven years has been content to play host to some three hundred boys at his Kamp OlympiK in New Jersey's Wharton Forest. He is also the athletic coach at Stockton State College.

Don, who was "motivated but not pressured" by his father, has high hopes for his two girls and two boys to excel in some field. "I don't care if it's playing baseball, crocheting, or interior decorating just so long as they set their minds on being the very best," he says.

He has had several operations on his legs and spine due to the punishment his body took while training, and he lives almost in constant pain. "What I accomplished would have been worth it," he says, even if it meant he had to spend the rest of his life in a wheelchair. He figures the tension he was under before the games took at least five years off his life.

Since the development of the fiber-glass pole, his record has been topped by almost three feet.

Outside his Kamp Olympik. *Antoinette Lopopolo*

A Hollywood career stymied by the McCarthy era.

MARSHA HUNT

The star who was once called "Hollywood's youngest character actress" was born Marcia Virginia Hunt on October 17, 1920, in Chicago. However, she was brought up in Manhattan, where she attended P.S. 9 and then the Horace Mann School. She helped pay for drama lessons by modeling for John Robert Powers.

At fifteen during a summer visit to her uncle in Los Angeles, two photographers who had worked with her in New York decided to trick Hollywood into putting her in pictures. They planted a story in the *Los Angeles Times,* which called her New York's No. 1 model. The article, which broke on page one of the second section, also stated that she had no interest whatever in a movie career. Neither statement was true. By noon, four studios had called her.

Marsha took the best offer, which was from Paramount, and made her first picture, *The Virginia Judge* (1935). There followed twelve almost identical parts playing "a sweet, simpering drip," but her strong complaints fell on deaf ears. After three years she left to free-lance for eighteen months before signing with M-G-M, where she spent six-and-a-half very happy years playing various roles.

For all the versatility she displayed in sixty-two features, she never fulfilled the potential many saw in her. One reason may be that her pictures were mostly B films, such as *Cheers for Miss Bishop* (1941), with William Gargan (living in Rancho La Costa, California), *Star Reporter* (1939), with Warren Hull (retired to Virginia Beach, Virginia), and *A Letter for Evie* (1945), with the late Spring Byington.[3] When the films were top quality, such as *Pride and Prejudice* (1940), *The Human Comedy* (1943), and *Smash-Up* (1947), they starred other performers. She was also in the memorable but unsuccessful *Actors and Sin* (1952), with the late Jenny Hecht.

One thing that greatly affected her was being told by David O. Selznick that she had the role of Melanie in *Gone With the Wind* only to read in the next day's paper that Olivia de Havilland had been signed. She vowed "never to let a professional disappointment matter that much to me again." Her resolution may have helped a decade later when she and her screen-writer-husband Robert Presnell were suspected of sympathizing with the Hollywood Ten; these refused to testify at the famous House Un-American Activities Committee hearings. The couple were no longer socially accept-able or hirable in many quarters.

Marsha appeared on Broadway in *The Devil's Disciple* and *Borned in Texas* in 1950, and in 1952 replaced Celeste Holm in *Affairs of State*.

After a trip around the world, however, she found her focus was more on humanist goals than on her career. She has devoted most of her time over the last years working for charities, such as for cerebral palsy, and as spokes-woman for some of the United Nations agencies.

In 1971, she played a small role in *Johnny Got His Gun,* her first feature in over eleven years. Though moving, it was a financial failure. During the 1972 season, she did a "Marcus Welby, M.D." segment.

Since their marriage in 1946, the Presnells have lived in their Sherman Oaks, California, rustic house. It is set on more than an acre of ground that includes a pool, tennis court, and lush rose garden next door to what was once the Buck Jones estate.

With her Malamute husky.
Ray Kozlowski

In 1955, Snooky was in his sixth year on "Your Hit Parade." *NBC*

SNOOKY LANSON

The star of television's "Hit Parade" was born on March 27, 1914, in Memphis, Tennessee, and was named Roy Landman. His mother soon started calling him "Snooky," which she took from the "Snooky Ookums" mentioned in an old Irving Berlin song. Mrs. Landman, who played several instruments, encouraged her son to take an interest in anything musical. As a little boy, he played at local benefit shows.

Snooky kicked around the music business for a number of years playing one-nighters, and for a while was the vocalist with a Mickey Mouse band that is well remembered today if only for its name—Cecil Golly and His Music By Golly! Then just before the United States entered the Second World War, Snooky's boyhood friend, Billy Schaeffer, began playing trombone with the Ray Noble (retired and living in Santa Barbara) orchestra. Schaeffer got Snooky a job after Noble's male singer took sick during a date in Cincinnati. The first thing Noble did was to shorten Snooky's last name to Lanson.

When Noble disbanded during the early part of the war, Snooky joined Al Donahue for a tour of one-nighters. Then he enlisted in the Naval Reserve for special service as Ted Weems's singer.

Snooky had cut some records with Ray Noble, such as "By the Light of the Silvery Moon" and "While My Lady Sleeps." But his first real hit came with "The Old Master Painter," which appeared on the best-seller charts in

1950. By then he had joined the cast of "Your Hit Parade," which was seen on television every Saturday evening during prime time. Though many performers with such exposure have been entirely forgotten, in a short time, "Snooky" registered, and he is known today by people who have never even seen him.

On the show, Lanson usually sang duets with Dorothy Collins,[3] and the two were the subject of a lot of fan-magazine gossip.

Snooky left "Your Hit Parade" in 1957 and he continued to make his home in Hartsdale, New York, while traveling about the country to play club dates and TV guest shots. In 1962 he moved to Atlanta where he hosted a variety program over WLWA-TV for two years. Then he spent two years living in Boca Raton, Florida, where he was able to do very well just working the hotels along the Gold Coast during the season. He had another variety show during 1966–67 on local television in Shreveport, Louisiana.

Since 1967 Snooky and Florence, his wife of thirty-four years, have been living in Nashville, Tennessee. They have three children: Ernie, a Marine Corps veteran who was wounded in Vietnam; Beth, who works for a Nashville insurance company; and Dan, still in school. Snooky works occasionally and was seen on the "Dick Cavett Show" along with Dorothy Collins in 1970. Most of the time, however, he is a salesman for a local Ford agency with the title of "special representative," which means that whenever show business calls he can take off for a while and it's okay with the boss.

Today he would like to sell all his fans a Ford. *Ben Bagley*

In *The Little Princess* (1939), one of her best.

MARCIA MAE JONES

The moppet character actress was born in Los Angeles on August 1, 1924. Her mother, who desperately wanted to be in movies, took Marcia on her rounds at the studios because she couldn't afford a baby-sitter. A casting director spotted Marcia, and she made her debut in *Mannequin* (1926), playing Dolores Costello[2] as a baby.

Most of the children brought to Hollywood in the heyday of kiddie stars during the 1930s were pretty, gay, and flirtatious. Marcia Mae, however, at an early age could project fear, sorrow, and vulnerability—feelings that were very much a part of her everyday life.

She had done a number of parts, such as in *The Champ* (1931), with Jackie Cooper, before William Wyler picked her for *These Three* (1936), the screen version of the Lillian Hellman hit play, *The Children's Hour*. In it, she played Rosalie, the shy, frightened little girl dominated by her older friend, played by Bonita Granville (Mrs. Jack Wrather and producer of TV's "Lassie" series). In 1937 Marcia had two major films in release, *Heidi*, with Shirley Temple, and *The Life of Emile Zola*, and followed with Deanna Durbin in *Mad About Music* (1938) and *First Love* (1939). Although *The Little Princess* (1939) was a Shirley Temple vehicle, many critics singled Marcia out for her outstanding performance. Some of Marcia's other pictures are *The Adventures of Tom Sawyer* (1938), with Tommy Kelly (an executive with the school board of Santa Ana, California), *Anne of Windy Poplars* (1940), with Anne Shirley (Mrs. Charles Lederer of Beverly Hills), *Nice Girl* (1941), *Top Man* (1943), with Susanna Foster,[3] *Snafu* (1946), and *The Daughter of Rosie O'Grady* (1950).

After her first marriage, to a lieutenant commander in the merchant marine ended in a 1951 divorce, she decided to quit acting for a while to devote more time to her two boys. For a time she was a receptionist in Greg Bautzer's law offices. From 1956 until 1963 Marcia was the wife of TV writer Bill Davenport. She made an occasional appearance on such TV shows as "The Cisco Kid" and "Wyatt Earp," but her personal problems sapped the energy she needed for a real comeback. Marcia has a degree in religious science and has completely conquered an alcohol problem that plagued her for years. The excellent work she did decades ago now stands out on the "Late Show" and has not gone unnoticed by casting directors. In 1972, old fans saw the adult Marcia Mae Jones on a segment of "Marcus Welby, M.D." and in the feature *The Spectre of Edgar Allan Poe.*

Marcia recalls her childhood in movies as a nightmare and has very strong feelings about children being encouraged to act. Her son Bob Chic, the stage manager on Dean Martin's TV show, was asked to test for the role of Boy in a Tarzan film some years ago. His mother flatly refused. She remembers: "I never seemed to fit anywhere. I wasn't like other kids and yet I wasn't an adult. The children in school took out their envy in ridicule. They wanted to be like me and I wanted to be like them."

Through analysis, she has come to understand and to forgive her mother. She hated her for years. "I've only recently begun to accept myself," she confessed. "My mother and I are now friends and I'm happy that she finally got what she wanted—a career." Her mother works constantly as an extra.

Today, in her apartment off the Sunset Strip. *Carl Robison*

The Andersons, 1960: Jane Wyatt, Robert Young, Billy Gray, Lauren Chapin, and Elinor Donahue.

BILLY GRAY

William Thomas Gray, the typical teen-ager of the fifties, was born on January 13, 1938, in Los Angeles. Just before his birth, his mother Beatrice, who had appeared in westerns with Bob Steele and Johnny Mack Brown,[3] was dropped from her R-K-O contract because she was pregnant and couldn't make a publicity tour with *New Faces of 1938,* her last film.

Billy was a precocious boy and began doing bit parts when he was only six years old. His first real role came in the 1946 M-G-M short, *Our Old Car,* one of the John Nesbitt *Passing Parade* series. Billy had a Warner Brothers contract and then moved over to Twentieth Century-Fox. He was seen in such features as *The Guy Who Came Back* (1951) and *By the Light of the Silvery Moon* (1953).

Gray's real fame came when he played Bud Anderson, son of Robert Young in the highly successful television series "Father Knows Best." He calls it "an embarrassment right from the beginning." Even a thirteen-year-old boy knew something was wrong when instead of the weekly $500 he had been getting in movies he was paid $250. And objections to a "Gosh" or "Golly" in his almost every line were dismissed without discussion. He settled down to what he felt was a real acting chore.

"Father" premiered over CBS on October 3, 1954, right in the middle of an era *McCall's* magazine dubbed "Togetherness," the desired state for the American family. The fictional insurance salesman, his wife, and three children from the small town of Springfield might have seemed close-knit on the screen, but not to Billy, who remembers that it was all strictly business and a lot of pretense.

162

On March 25, 1962, about a year after production had ceased on the series, Billy was stopped by police on suspicion of drunk driving. Gray admits that he has smoked marijuana but certainly not that night, nor had he anything to drink. The officers, however, found a small amount of marijuana seeds and stems under the front seat of his car and the story hit every newspaper in the country. The actor drew a three-month jail term and was on probation for three years afterward. He found that upon his release he was persona non grata around the studios, and his agent explained that he didn't feel he would be able to represent him anymore. As for those from the old TV series, the only one who contacted him was the prop man.

Gray traveled for a while, bought some income property in the Topanga Canyon section of Los Angeles, and settled down, with a woman, for eight years. They were married for the last two years but have since been divorced.

Billy has no regrets about being a child actor except for the studio schools. They were so lax, he claims he is still learning to read and write properly. However, what he recalls with some pain is that he would have been in the James Dean starrer *Rebel Without a Cause* (1955) had the producers of his TV series agreed to shoot around him for two weeks.

Billy is confident about his future as an actor. He played a drug dealer in the unsuccessful film *Dusty and Sweets McGee* (1971) and is now planning a picture with his friend Jack Nicholson. Although he is often complimented on the good performances he turned in on all those "Father Knows Best" episodes, he winces whenever the show is mentioned. It particularly bothers him that young people are still seeing the half-hour programs; they continue in syndication all around the country. "I'm so ashamed," he says, "that I had any part in all that. I wish there was some way I could tell kids not to believe it—the dialogue, the situations, the characters—they were all totally false."

Billy in the woods surrounding his Topanga Canyon house. *Paul Schaeffer*

With Eleanore Whitney, teamed in *Turn Off the Moon* (1937).

JOHNNY DOWNS

"Joe College" of the movies was born in Brooklyn on October 13, 1913. His Navy father took the family to Coronado, California, where Johnny began appearing in amateur shows, playing violin and doing patter. His mother, who had his hair cut to look like Jackie Coogan's, got him a bit part in a Charlie Chase short. When a director spotted him, he told her that if she cut his bangs he would put him in an "Our Gang" comedy. Johnny appeared in the silent two-reelers along with Farina, Mary Kornman, and Fat Joe Cobb (living in Los Angeles) at a beginning salary of $50 a week in 1924.

By the time he left in 1926 to tour the vaudeville circuits with Mary Kornman he was making $60 a week. That act broke up after two years and Johnny worked sporadically as a single until he replaced Jack Whiting in the Los Angeles company of Olsen and Johnson's *Take a Chance* in 1933.

M-G-M gave him a screen test that was shown to Paramount, for whom he appeared in the college musicals then the rage. Though Johnny has never been to college, he has played the collegian in such films as *College Rhythm* (1934), *College Scandal* (1935) with Arline Judge (living in Hollywood), *Pigskin Parade* (1936), *Hold That Co-ed* (1938) with Marjorie Weaver (owner of a liquor store in West Los Angeles), and *All American Co-ed* (1941) with Frances Langford.[2] Even when he wasn't playing the big man on campus, Johnny was in pictures slated for the youth market: *Thrill of a*

Lifetime (1937) and *Parents on Trial* (1939). He was paired with Eleanore Whitney (Mrs. Frederick Backer of Manhattan) in a number of features such as *Blonde Trouble* (1937); the publicity department had them linked romantically. Few people remember that he ever played anything but enthusiastic young men. But he was a member of Charles Boyer's gang of thieves in *Algiers* (1938) and was Susan Hayward's husband in *Adam Had Four Sons* (1941). Even after *The Mad Monster* (1942), with the late Anne Neagle, he couldn't shake his image.

Throughout the forties his type of movie was out of vogue and he went to Broadway for two musicals, *Are You with It?* (1945) and *Hold It* (1948). Although he had a part in the prestigious feature *Rhapsody in Blue* (1945), by 1950 Johnny was reduced to working in a Rex Allen western, *Hills of Oklahoma*. When he accepted an offer to work as an announcer on a San Diego TV station in 1953, he was a stand-in for Dean Martin during dance sequences. With the same station, within months he took over the hosting chores on a kiddie show that became extremely popular in the area. Thanks to a boy and four girls of his own, he had an easy rapport with his audience and continued on the program until it went off the air in 1971. Johnny's youngest daughter, Reene, is a cheerleader at Coronado High School.

The young man who used to date Dixie Dunbar and Judy Garland has been married since 1941 and is a devout Roman Catholic. He sells real estate now but has by no means closed the door to a comeback. "I can still dance a little," says Johnny, "and if the right thing comes along we could be packed in no time."

Mollie (*left*) and Reene (*right*) Downs with their dad in Coronado, California. *Jerry Mastroli*

In the late thirties she starred in three vehicles for Republic Pictures.

FRIEDA INESCORT

The handsome character actress of stage and screen was born Frieda Wightman on June 29, 1901, in Edinburgh, Scotland. Her father was a journalist and her mother was Elaine Inescourt, a well-known actress.

Frieda worked in London as confidential secretary to Lady Astor before coming to New York in 1919. For a short time she was with the National Child Labor Commission and then became a secretary at the British Consulate. One night in 1921 after seeing *The Dover Road* she went backstage to congratulate some friends in the cast. They encouraged her to try acting. So she asked for an appointment with the producer, Winthrop Ames, who mistook her name for her mother's. But he offered Frieda a part in *The Truth About Blayds* (1922). She and the play went over very well, but her mother, who had objected to her acting, deeply resented Frieda's success. For years she had introduced Frieda as her sister.

She continued working ten to four and, even after runs in *You and I* (1923) and *Hay Fever* (1925), accepted a job as publicity director for G. P. Putnam, the publishers. Only after marrying critic-poet Ben Ray Redman in 1926 did she commit herself fully to acting. Frieda played opposite Leslie Howard in *Escape* (1927) and *Springtime for Henry* (1931) before moving to Hollywood in 1935.

Her first film was *Dark Angel* (1935), followed in the next year by five features, including *The Great O'Malley* with Sybil Jason (married and living in Hollywood). Many people expected Frieda to become a star. Republic Pictures made a valiant attempt with three vehicles: *Portia on Trial* (1937), *Woman Doctor* (1939), with Henry Wilcoxon, and *Zero*

166

Hour (1939). In them she played career women and got good notices. But the studio was not a prestige operation, and they did only fair at the box office. Warner Brothers put her under contract and then dropped her after only six months. In *The Letter* (1940), she was photographed from an angle aimed at preventing her from taking the scene from Bette Davis. (Frieda learned later that Warner's signed her only to frighten Kay Francis into line.)

She continued to work in such pictures as *Convicted Woman* (1940), with June Lang (living in North Hollywood), *Remember the Day* (1941), *The Amazing Mrs. Holliday* (1943), and *The Return of the Vampire* (1944). In 1944, she returned to Broadway for *Soldier's Wife*. Among her last credits are *The Judge Steps Out* (1949), *Never Wave at a Wac* (1952), and *Flame of the Islands* (1955), with Barbara O'Neil (living in Cos Cob, Connecticut).

However, her Hollywood career had been preceded by a fateful event. One night in 1932, on stage in her greatest success, *When Ladies Meet*, she could not complete a line. Her costar, Walter Abel, covered for her. It was the first symptom of her incurable disease—multiple sclerosis. She fought it for years through exercise and will power, never telling anyone but her physician. But in recent years it has taken such a toll that she is confined to a wheelchair at the Motion Picture Country Hospital in Woodland Hills, California.

As an actress, Frieda was at her best in roles requiring great dignity, such as in *Pride and Prejudice* (1940), and class consciousness, as in *A Place in the Sun* (1951). But in real life, she is relaxed and amusing, and she loathes pretensions of any kind. She considers her greatest successs the thirty-five years of happiness she knew with her husband. He died on August 1, 1961. She receives as much, sometimes more, fan mail as anyone at the retreat, but her condition prevents her from replying.

Now living at the Motion Picture Country Hospital. *Michael Knowles*

He headlined the Palace Theatre's last week of vaudeville in November, 1932.

NICK LUCAS

The "Singing Troubadour" was born in Newark, New Jersey, on August 22, 1897. He played the guitar in grade school and by his teens had mastered mandolin and banjo as well—and earned money locally playing for parties and weddings.

After graduation, with the Kentucky Five, a group that featured Nick, the leader, and Ted Fio Rito, on piano, he played clubs and toured vaudeville houses for two years before joining the Vernon Country Club Band in New York, playing guitar. In joining this group, he is credited by many people as being the first to replace the banjo with guitar. Another first attributed to him is the introduction of the six-string guitar to popular music.

After the Armistice, Lucas toured the Continent and appeared at London's Kit Kat Club and Café de Paris. Upon his return to the United States he signed on with Ted Fio Rito, who was becoming a name as the leader of the Oriole Orchestra at Chicago's Edgewater Beach Hotel. Their performances were broadcast over radio, with no payment to the musicians since at that time there were practically no commercials on radio and no way to measure the audience the then infant medium was reaching. It was at this stand that Nick began singing, and the mail poured in. Brunswick Records got word of his popularity and signed him to a recording contract in 1925. His first record was "My Best Girl." Overnight, it began to get him top money in vaudeville houses around the country, and he followed up with "Dancing with Tears in My Eyes," "Among My Souvenirs," and "When You Wore a Tulip."

In 1929 Nick made two highly successful and historically important features for Warner Brothers. In *Gold Diggers of Broadway,* one of the first all-talkie musicals, Nick warbled "Painting the Clouds with Sunshine," which he expected to be the big hit of the production. It was a hit all right, but

168

nothing to compare with his other number, "Tip-Toe Thru' the Tulips With Me," which he sang while chorus girls pranced through a field of artificial tulips. The song has been associated with him ever since. Both his sequences in the film were in early Technicolor. In the all-star *Show of Shows* he sang "Li-Po-Li" to Myrna Loy, who was made up to look Chinese.

Although Lucas made only one other feature, *Disc Jockey*, a 1951 cheapie, in the early thirties he appeared in a number of shorts for Warner's and Universal. Warner's had offered him a contract after his first movie success, but he chose to continue in vaudeville where he was commanding $2,000 a week. The studio therefore signed a young man from Pittsburgh, Dick Powell.

Despite the Depression, Lucas did quite well and had his own radio series for several seasons during the thirties. Of course, vaudeville was hit hard at this time, but he remained one of the big draws. When the famed Palace Theatre ended its stage policy, in November, 1932, Nick was on the closing bill, along with Hal Le Roy.[3]

Beginning in 1948 he was with Ken Murray's Blackouts in Hollywood, for one hundred straight weeks. When Tiny Tim began to click in the late 1960s, Nick was back in the picture: the new star during all his many talk show appearances spoke of how Lucas had inspired him. At Tim's request he came to New York from Hollywood for Tim's famous TV wedding; on December 17, 1969, Nick sang "Tip-Toe Thru' the Tulips" before the largest audience in TV history.

Nick has never stopped working and is offered far more bookings than the few he accepts, such as at Harrah's Club, in Reno, and at conventions. The Nick Lucas guitar, perhaps the first personalized instrument in the world, introduced in 1925, has provided him with royalties for many years. The guitar pick, which is named after him, is still a top seller.

Nick's wife of fifty-three years died in 1970, but he has a daughter and three grandsons. He visits them often at their ranch in Colorado. He lives alone just off Hollywood Boulevard in the same apartment building as does his costar from *Show of Shows,* Jack Mulhall.

Beside the pool of his Hollywood apartment house. *Claude Wagner*

In 1938, appearing in *Girls' School.*

DORIS KENYON

The silent star and talkies leading lady was born in Syracuse, New York, on September 5, 1897. Her father, a writer and publisher, and the protégé of Henry Wadsworth Longfellow, was a friend of Teddy Roosevelt.

One night at the Authors Club Victor Herbert heard Doris sing, and he gave her a small part in his musical *Princess Pat* (1915). A movie producer spotted her and she began making features, such as *The Man Who Stood Still* (1916) and the serial *The Hidden Hand* (1917) with Arlene Pretty (single and living in Hollywood).

By the mid-twenties, Doris not only was a well-established and important movie star; she had enormous prestige through her continuing success on Broadway. Between such of her pictures as *The Ruling Passion* (1922), with George Arliss, and *Born Rich* (1924), with Cullen Landis (living in Cheboygan, Michigan), Doris appeared on stage in such vehicles as *The Girl in the Limousine* (1919), *The White Villa* (1921), and *The Gift* (1924). She was opposite Rudolph Valentino in *Monsieur Beaucaire* (1924) and now says of the great lover: "He wasn't my type but he was attractive, I suppose—for a Latin." She continued through the silent period making such features as *Men of Steel* (1926) and *Burning Daylight* (1928).

When sound came in, to be past thirty was an insurmountable drawback to most of her contemporaries. But Doris's first film, *Interference* (1928), was a big hit. When her husband, silent star Milton Sills, died suddenly in 1930, she talked of retiring. But her old friend George Arliss insisted she be his leading lady in *Alexander Hamilton* (1931) and in *Voltaire* (1933). She was also with John Barrymore in *Counsellor-at-Law* (1933). Her second and third marriages ended in divorce.

During the 1930s Doris began to intersperse her movie work with concert recitals and spent two years in Europe singing and studying with the legendary Yvette Guilbert. She also began writing magazine articles, with much success, but for a new audience—the middle-aged woman. Although Doris left films after *The Man in the Iron Mask* (1939), she sang a great deal during the Second World War for the USO and lectured and sang for women's groups. In 1947 she became the wife of Bronislaw Mylnarski, a music expert and brother-in-law of Artur Rubinstein. She made a few TV appearances as late as the 1960s, but they were favors for friends, Efrem Zimbalist, Jr., and Walter Brennan. And with Bronislaw, she entertained and traveled a great deal, until he died in 1971. That same year her only child, Kenyon Sills, died suddenly. He was forty-five.

Doris shows little interest in her theatrical career but she is pleased to learn that she is remembered: "It's nice to know I gave some pleasure to some people." She lives with her teen-age grandson in a French country-style house in Beverly Hills complete with an aviary of white doves, two pet squirrels, and a heated pool she swims in nude daily.

Beside a painting of her late son. *All-Together Enterprises*

"PEPPER YOUNG'S FAMILY"

"Pepper Young's Family" began on the National Broadcasting Company on October 2, 1932, but at that time it was called "Red Adams." The title character was played by Burgess Meredith, who was just beginning to make a name for himself. He shortly left the cast to do a Broadway play, which led to his Hollywood career. The program was soon sponsored by Beech-Nut Gum. But they insisted that since Adams was the name of a competitive chewing gum, it would have to be changed. It was—to "Red Davis." That didn't last long either, and the third title was "Forever Young." That seemed to conflict with Gloria Swanson's line of dresses designed for women middle-aged and beyond. Finally, they agreed on the title that lasted until the final broadcast on January 7, 1959.

The late Elaine Carrington, who became known in her profession as the "Queen of the Soap Operas," was the creator of the durable series, which was one of the best written and most believable of all of the daytime serials of radio's Golden Age.

The main character of Larry "Pepper" Young was taken over by the late Curtis Arnall when Meredith left. Lawson Zerbe (living in Manhattan and still active in radio and TV) was Pepper Young No. 3, leaving in 1945 to go into the service. Mason Adams, who had just been discharged from the Army, auditioned for the role. But by the time Adams learned that he had the part, he had already signed with the Chicago company to do the play *Dear Ruth*. He got his release from *Ruth* only after he had found another actor to play the role. Adams took on Pepper admittedly for the money. He felt contempt for radio acting. It still embarrasses him. But he played the part to the end of the show's radio run.

Pepper on the air aged about one year in every four; he was the editor of the local newspaper in the small town of Elmwood; the state or region was never defined but the show's customs, accents, and personalities were definitely Middle American. The Youngs were typified as registered Republicans who voted for FDR at least for the first and second terms. They were more threatened than hurt by the Depression and they managed throughout to keep a live-in maid, named Hattie Williams, who was played by Greta Kvalden (now Mrs. Gilmore and retired from acting and living in Manhattan). "Money," says Mason today, "was something we never talked about."

So popular was the soap that for a while it was heard not only twice a day (once in the morning and, the same script again, in the afternoon) but on both the NBC and CBS networks—simultaneously. Each episode began with the announcer, either Martin Block or Alan Kent, saying: "Now it's time again for a visit with your friends, the Youngs." The theme music at the beginning and end was "Au Matin." But the sponsor most closely identified with the program was Camay, at the time called "the soap of beautiful women."

For most of its years on the air, Sam Young, Pepper's father, was played by Thomas Chalmers, who has since died, as has Marion Barney, who played his wife. Pepper married his childhood sweetheart, Linda Benton, who was acted by Eunice Howard (now residing in Roxbury, Connecticut). Adams still sees Chick Vincent, who was his director for so many years. Occasionally he sees Betty Wragge, who played sister Peggy from the very first show. Miss Wragge lives in Manhattan and was Ruby Keeler's understudy in the Broadway musical *No, No, Nanette*.

Few actors from radio soaps have fared better than Mason Adams. His voice is heard on so many commercials that he declines to name some for fear of offending the others. Nevertheless, for many years Mason has been official spokesman for Smucker's jams and jellies on all their radio and TV advertising.

Adams lives in Westport, Connecticut, with his wife and their son and daughter. Although he was born in New York City, his voice is as Middle West in tone and pattern as Henry Fonda's. To this day it is still recognized, and always as Pepper Young's—even by audiences that have seen him play the prosecuting attorney in the play *Inquest* in 1970, the father in *You Know I Can't Hear You When the Water's Running*, in the London company, in 1968, and the judge in *The Trial of the Catonsville 9* in 1971. When he ordered a cup of coffee at a diner recently in Toronto, the waitress said, "I know that voice. You're Pepper Young!"

Mason Adams when he took over the role of Pepper in April, 1945. *NBC*

Today a very active New York actor. *Diana Keyt*

The Sweetest Girl in the Movies, 1934.

MARY BRIAN

"The sweetest girl in pictures" was born Louise Dantzler on February 17, 1908, in Corsicana, Texas, and brought up in Dallas. Her father died when she was a month old. Her mother then moved with her son and daughter to Hollywood in 1923, where Mary met one of the heads of Paramount. The studio was then looking for young, unfamiliar faces to play in its production of *Peter Pan* (1925). Her college teacher mother was unimpressed with the profession of acting, but allowed Mary to be placed under contract for seven years.

The film was a huge success and made Mary and the other two players, the late Betty Bronson[3] and Esther Ralston,[2] overnight stars. The children who came to see Mary on her public appearance tours were disappointed when she couldn't fly as she did on screen.

Mary made as many as seven features a year for her studio, *Beau Geste* (1926), *Harold Teen* (1928), and *The Virginian* (1929), among them. She attended school on the Paramount lot with other child actors, including Phillippe de Lacy (an executive with an advertising agency in Los Angeles). She thoroughly enjoyed her work and the people she met, but she never developed a driving ambition or an extravagant life-style.

The advent of sound didn't panic her and she survived easily, making quite a few talkies, among them the impressive *Royal Family of Broadway* (1930) and *The Front Page* (1931). Jimmy Cagney was her leading man in *Hard to Handle* (1933), Lanny Ross[1] crooned to her in *College Rhythm*

(1934), and W. C. Fields played her dad in *The Man on the Flying Trapeze* (1935). Nothing she did on film contradicted "the sweetest girl in pictures" image until she played a shrew in *The Spendthrift* (1936), with Henry Fonda. But by then her career was on such a decline, her only offers came from England, where she went for three features. It meant leaving the big love of her life, Dick Powell, with whom she was linked for about two years.

Mary returned to the United States in the late 1930s, playing presentation houses with two boys in a dancing act, and she entertained GIs in Europe and North Africa a good deal during World War II. She made *No Escape* (1943) for low-budget Monogram studios and then even went one step lower to PRC for *Women at Work* (1943) before calling it quits. She came back for thirty-nine weeks in 1955, playing the mother in the "Meet Corliss Archer" TV series.

Six years after her marriage to artist Jon Whitcomb for all of three months and two days in 1941, Mary wed George Tomasini, the film editor who cut many of Alfred Hitchcock's movies, including *North By Northwest* and *Psycho*.

A widow since 1967, Mary lives with her two puli dogs in her Studio City beamed-ceiling ranch-style house surrounded by woods. Her hobby, which has proved very profitable, is painting famous people (e.g., Conrad Hilton and Red Skelton).

She doesn't completely rule out acting again in movies. But the one real chance she had to become a star again was when she tested for the lead in *A Star Is Born* (1937). "It was almost a disappointment," says Mary now. "I say 'almost' because when I saw Janet Gaynor in the picture I saw at once that she was the one who was meant to get it. She was absolutely wonderful!"

With two of her pulis.

Under contract to Twentieth Century-Fox, 1941.

REGINALD GARDINER

The "frightfully" British comedian was born on February 27, 1903, in Wimbledon, Surrey, England, to upper-middle-class parents who provided him with a good education. It ended in 1923 when he graduated with honors from London's Royal Academy of Dramatic Art.

Reggie dropped a first name, William, when he made the rounds of London's West End. He had it relatively easy from the beginning, and landed a part as a walk-on in *The Prisoner of Zenda* (1923). He worked regularly in England, doing such plays as *Old Heidelberg* (1925), *Blackmail* (1928), and *Chance Acquaintance* (1928), and added films—*The Lodger* (1928) and *How's Chances?* (1934)—that he claims "no one I have ever met has seen."

He was handsome and funny. Broadway audiences were delighted with his "imitation of wall paper" in *At Home Abroad* (1935), with Eddie Foy (living in Sherman Oaks, California). He was back again the next year, his second appearance with his friend Bea Lillie (living on East End Avenue in New York City), in *The Show Is On,* which also featured Eleanor Powell.[2]

The Reginald Gardiner brand of urbane wit also clicked with U.S. movie audiences, right from the start. He made three musicals: *Born to Dance* (1936), *A Damsel in Distress* (1937), and *Everybody Sing* (1938), followed by the lavish Norma Shearer[2] starrer, *Marie Antoinette* (1938).

He worked for most of the major studios, doing among others *The Girl Downstairs* (1939), with Franciska Gaal (the late Mrs. Francis de Dajkovich of Manhattan), *Dulcy* (1940), *The Man Who Came to Dinner* (1941), and *Captains of the Clouds* (1942), his favorite, before settling down to a long Twentieth Century-Fox contract. Of his typecasting he says: "Zanuck knew what he wanted. We all knew better than to suggest anything, much less object."

Reggie made a great many appearances for the USO during World War II, and did the films Hollywood considered lifted civilian and military morale, such as *Sweet Rosie O'Grady* (1943) and *The Dolly Sisters* (1945). *Molly and Me* (1945), which was supposed to launch Gracie Fields in America, didn't seem to lift anyone's morale and was one of the year's box-office disasters. Reggie made *Cluny Brown* (1946) and *The Halls of Montezuma,* and was then reunited with Bea Lillie for *An Evening With Bea Lillie* on Broadway in 1952. He remained for the long tour that followed.

In 1954 he was seen in *The Barefoot Contessa;* also *The Black Widow,* in which he was a suspected murderer. "Wouldn't you know that it turns out I didn't do it?" laments Gardiner. "Even in *The Great Dictator* [1940], the Nazi I played was a nice Nazi!"

After *Around the World in 80 Days* (1956), he made only two features: *Back Street* (1961) and *Sergeant Deadhead* (1965).

He guested on many TV shows and for a season had his own series, "The Pruitts of South Hampton," in 1966–67.

Several years ago the debonair actor fell down the stairs of his Beverly Hills home and injured his head so seriously that it has impaired his vocabulary and balance. About the same time he and Nadya Petrova, his wife since 1942, separated, and Reggie moved to Manhattan where he lives alone in an apartment overlooking Columbus Circle. He watches TV and paints, examples of which adorn the walls of his apartment. He goes out very little, and never alone, but when he does venture onto New York streets he is pleased by how many people, particularly the young, recognize him.

Of his life now, he says: It is "so much easier for me than it would be for most actors. I'm a ham, of course, and I'd love to work again but sitting about doing nothing all day, well, in my case it's like working. I just pretend I'm playing another lounge lizard."

The author and Reggie in the actor's Manhattan apartment. *Kaj Donau*

In a scene from her one big bid for stardom, Cecil B. de Mille's *The Godless Girl* (1929).

LINA BASQUETTE

The "Screen Tragedy Girl" (as dubbed by Adela Rogers St. Johns) was born Lena Baskette on April 19, 1907, in San Mateo, California. At the San Francisco World's Fair of 1915, as a Baby Ballerina, she was the featured attraction for the Victor Talking Machine Co.'s exhibition. Then Carl Laemmle, Sr., got her father drunk and signed her to a long-term contract with his Universal Pictures, at $50 a week. Along with the *Lena Baskette Featurettes,* she ground out such features as *Shoes* (1916) and *Penrod* (1922).

In 1917, a year after her father died, her mother married dance director Ernest Belcher; their daughter—Lena's half sister—is Marge Champion. Her mother, who ranks among the legendary stage mothers of all time, aided by Belcher's coaching, got Lena into the *Ziegfeld Follies of 1923*. She was billed third, as "America's Prima Ballerina." John Murray Anderson, who was with Ziegfeld at the time, changed her name to Lina Basquette.

Anna Pavlova, after seeing her dance to "A Pretty Girl Is Like a Melody," offered to make Lina her protégée. But Mrs. Belcher preferred large salaries to the prestige of the ballet. She even put her daughter in the shows at Texas Guinan's speakeasy after her *Follies* performances, until Ziegfeld strongly objected.

Lina encouraged Sam Warner, whom she married in 1925, to pursue his interest in sound films and she was instrumental in getting him to star Al Jolson in *The Jazz Singer* (1927). After Sam died, in 1927, she unwittingly signed away most of her inheritance and then her in-laws waged a three-year siege of legal harassments over custody of her daughter, Lita. Front-page stories in 1930 reported how the little girl was finally taken from her mother by the Warners, and of Lina's attempted suicide.

In spite of her domestic crisis, Cecil B. De Mille starred her in the ill-fated *Godless Girl* (1929). It most likely would have made her a big star but by the time it was released the public was no longer interested in silents.

There followed a torrid and complicated affair with Jack Dempsey, which ended with her second suicide attempt, in 1932. Lina was married at the time to the fighter's trainer.

The Warners were hostile to the idea of her working in pictures but she still managed to work in westerns with Buck Jones and Hoot Gibson, plus some B's such as *Morals for Women* (1931), *Midnight Lady* (1932), with Johnny Darrow (residing in Malibu, California, where he writes a newspaper column), *The Final Hour* (1936), and *Four Men and a Prayer* (1938).

From 1937 to 1939 she toured the world in such plays as *Black Limelight* and *Idiot's Delight*. After returning to the United States, she made her last movie, *A Night for Crime* (1942).

In August of 1943 she brought charges of rape and assault against a twenty-two-year-old United States Army private, who was found guilty and sentenced to twenty years in prison.

Since 1949 Lina has been the owner of Honey Hollow Kennels, a twenty-five-acre estate in Chalfont, Bucks County, Pennsylvania, where she raises the Great Danes that have taken more prizes at dog shows in every category than has any other Great Dane kennel in the country. Among the famous who own Basquette Danes are Raymond Burr, Mike Nichols, and the Crown Prince of Iraq.

Lina is a grandmother by her son, a retired Marine, who owns a restaurant in Yuma, Arizona. She has heard from her daughter only a few times since she was taken from her over forty years ago. Lina readily admits that she is a very different person from the one who enlivened newspapers during the 1930s with her colorful personal life. She said recently that after six husbands she thinks she knows what it takes to make a good marriage— "Now that nobody's interested!" she adds with a laugh.

With Kimboyh, one of her many prize-winning Great Danes.
Martin Booth

In 1932, with Madge Evans
(now Mrs. Sidney Kingsley).

WILLIAM HAINES

The perennial smart aleck of the movies was born in Virginia on January 1, 1900. He was educated at the Staunton Military School there and sang in the choir of the local Episcopal church, until he ran away in 1914.

For the next few years. Haines worked at a variety of jobs, in a rubber factory, a powder plant, and in the office of S. W. Strauss as an assistant bookkeeper. He was an office boy on Wall Street when Robert B. McIntyre, casting director for Samuel Goldwyn, saw him on the street one day. He entered William in the Goldwyn-sponsored New Faces contest. He and Eleanor Boardman (now living in Santa Barbara, California) were the winners. They were put under contract and sent to Hollywood where Haines made his debut in *Brothers Under the Skin* (1922).

Although he was generally dismissed by the critics as obnoxious and an impertinent pretty boy, his pictures did well at the box office. In most of them he played the wisecracking young man who turns out to be honorable in a crisis and true-blue when it comes to the girl, whom he always got in the last reel. Along with his large, loyal moviegoing following, his popularity within the movie colony was an important factor in his career. He was a great favorite at Hollywood parties for his quick and bitchy wit, and also popular with fan magazines for his photogenic features and fashionable lifestyle.

Before his popularity began to wane in the early thirties, William was seen in dozens of films, among them *Three Wise Fools* (1923), *Circe, The Enchantress* (1924), *Brown of Harvard* (1926), *Tell It to the Marines* (1927), with Esther Ralston,[2] *Alias Jimmy Valentine* (1928), M-G-M's first venture into talkies, *The Duke Steps Out* (1929), with Eddie Nugent

180

(living on Manhattan's Mitchell Place), *The Girl Said No* (1930), and *The Fast Life* (1932), with Madge Evans (now the wife of playwright Sidney Kingsley).

When the subject of careers ruined by scandal comes up William Haines's name is invariably mentioned. Actually Haines was finished in movies before such troubles. His swan song was in *The Marines Are Coming,* released in 1934. By then he was well established as an interior decorator. Four years earlier with his friend Jimmy Shields they set up an antique and decorating shop, which did well thanks to commissions from such close friends as his former costar Joan Crawford. It was in June of 1936 that Haines, Shields, and over a dozen male friends were beaten, pelted with garbage, and literally driven out of the beach town of El Porto by a group of some one hundred townspeople who called themselves the White Legion. The parents of a six-year-old boy accused a member of the party of molesting their child. No charges were ever brought by either side but front-page newspaper stories at the time screamed the details of how Haines had had both eyes blackened.

Haines dislikes personal publicity and prefers to talk about his decorating rather than his acting career when interviewed. Over the years his prestige as an interior decorator has risen steadily in Southern California where he has put his touch on such interiors as that of the old Mocambo club and the lavish new Jack Warner estate. Although the London press was critical of his work recently for U.S. Ambassador Annenberg, he seemed to please the multimillionaire diplomat who spent about $1 million in decorating and refurbishing the embassy.

Haines, who has referred to his movie image as "the world's oldest college boy," is considered a great social catch among Hollywood's old guard. He and director George Cukor—long noted for his instincts about moviedom's ever-changing pecking order—have been friends for years. Haines does quite a bit of entertaining himself in his elaborate Brentwood home, which he has greatly expanded from its humble FHA beginnings.

The interior decorator today. *Jon Virzi*

In 1933 Zita made *Luxury Liner* with George Brent.

ZITA JOHANN

The dramatic star of stage and films was born near Temesvar, Hungary, on July 14, 1904. When she was seven, her father, who had been an officer in the Emperor's Hussars, brought the family to the United States.

After excelling in acting at Bryant High School on Long Island, she made the rounds of casting offices and auditions until Basil Sydney chose her as his leading woman in the Theatre Guild Acting Company. She played in *He Who Gets Slapped, Peer Gynt,* and *The Devil's Disciple* on the 1923–24 tour. After that, she did *Dawn* (1925) and had the title role in *Aloma of the South Seas* (1925).

Zita wore clothes well, had a beautifully modulated, authoritative voice, and was considered a young actress with great promise. But she had also developed a reputation for voicing ideas about truth in acting, and the hamminess of the day was not her style. Long before the Method was known to Broadway actors, she used music for moods before a curtain. She disagreed over the interpretation of her part in *Lost* (1927) and was fired from the play, but not before Arthur Hopkins caught a performance. He offered her the starring role in *Machinal* (1928). To accept, she had to turn down the lead in the movie version of *Show Boat*—and a lucrative five-year contract that went with it. It was worth it. Critics took little notice of *Machinal's* leading man, an unknown Clark Gable, and gave her raves.

M-G-M wanted her so badly in 1929 they gave her a contract with script approval. But when she refused them, first *The Thirteenth Chair* and then *East Lynne,* they dropped her option. She returned to Broadway and had such a hit in *To-Morrow and To-Morrow* (1931) she was unable to star in *Alien Corn,* written for her by Sidney Kingsley.

D. W. Griffith chose her for his first talkie, *The Struggle* (1931) but it was a failure. She began depending on her husband, John Houseman, for advice, who at the time had no theatrical experience. She signed a five-year contract with R-K-O. When they offered her *Thirteen Women*, she asked for her release. Universal signed her for *Laughing Boy*, but it was never made. Houseman insisted she do *The Mummy* (1933) and *Luxury Liner* (1933), with his constant refrain: "It's more money than you could ever make in the theatre." Her other pictures were *Tiger Shark* (1932), *The Sin of Norma Moran* (1933), and *Grand Canary* (1934).

She returned to Broadway in such so-so vehicles as *Waltz in Fire* (1934), *Panic* (1935), *The Burning Deck* (1940), and *Broken Journey* (1942).

Since 1939 Zita has lived in a large pre-Revolutionary house on eight wooded acres in West Nyack, New York. She works almost daily with teen-agers who are considering a career in the theatre; also with younger, disadvantaged children. She has had remarkable results with both groups, but particularly with deaf mutes; at least one mute, though retarded as well, has learned to speak and hear. From these sessions the childless former star has fashioned a TV series, which will be directed and produced by Ed Franck. It is scheduled for syndication this year.

That an actress with such a memorable presence and style so far ahead of her time should be remembered chiefly for her role in the classic horror film *The Mummy*, is as sad as it is curious. Zita may have answered the question in a recent interview when she spoke of her three unsuccessful marriages. Miss Johann, dubbed by her mentor "the candor kid," said: "I think I chose the men I did because I felt I could hold my own with them. Now that it's too late I realize you can only hold your own with nice people."

In the woods near home in West Nyack, New York. *Michael Knowles*

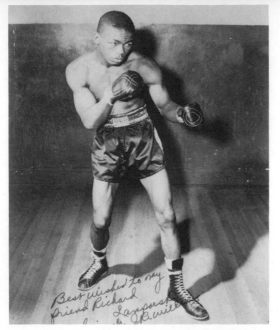

In 1948 named Fighter of the Year.

IKE WILLIAMS

The former Lightweight Boxing Champion of the World was born in Brunswick, Georgia, on August 2, 1923. When he was nine years old, his parents separated and his mother brought him to live in Trenton, New Jersey. He had his share of fights with boys in the neighborhood, but Ike's first awareness of professional boxing was in January, 1933, when he read the obituary of James J. Corbett.

Ike started working out at the local YMCA, where the boys shortened his first name, Isaiah, to Ike. In 1939 he began entering amateur contests but won only two of the five he fought in. After turning pro in 1940, however, his average improved greatly, and some of the more important matchmakers regarded him as a comer.

For five years, beginning in 1943, the lightweight boxing crown was in dispute. Between the New York Boxing Commission and the National Boxing Association feud, it was difficult to tell whether the title rightfully belonged to Beau Jack, Bob Montgomery, Sammy Angott, Juan Zurita, or Williams. Ike settled it all when, satisfying all parties concerned, he stepped into the ring with Bob Montgomery on August 4, 1947. He had met Montgomery before, when on January 25, 1944, Montgomery KO'd him in the twelfth round after giving him a bad beating. It was the only time in Ike's career that he had a personal dislike for an opponent, and it was with great personal—as well as professional—satisfaction that he took the title, which was recognized by everyone.

1948 was Ike's big year. He successfully defended his title three times, was named Fighter of the Year, beat Beau Jack, and, for conquering Enrique Bolonas, was paid the largest purse of his career—$50,000. Ike's contract granted him two-thirds of his earnings after expenses.

Ike, whose offer to give Patty de Marco a shot at the title was declined, rates Kid Gavalan as the best man he ever met in the ring. He considers Sugar Ray Robinson the greatest fighter of all time, although he refused a match with him since Robinson outweighed him by fifteen pounds.

He claims that just before his fight with Jimmy Carter on May 25, 1951, he was offered a large sum of money to take a dive. He refused, but during training he injured his right shoulder. Although at the time he never mentioned that he had been hurt, he now maintains that he lost the crown to Carter because of that injury.

Six months later, Ike, who had a wife and three children, took his girl friend to visit Joe Louis (now a greeter at Caesar's Palace in Las Vegas), who was training for his bout with Marciano. Louis said to him: "Look at you. You lost the title and now you're going to lose everything!" Williams never handled very well the fame or money that accompanied his title. He was known in sporting circles as a big spender, and any investments he made turned out badly. And some of his closest friends during those years found him unbearably arrogant.

Within four years of Louis's comment, Williams had been defeated in nearly all his ten matches, and his wife had left him. He was last in the ring with Beau Jack (owner of the shoeshine concession at the Fontainebleau Hotel in Miami Beach), who defeated him on August 18, 1955.

In 1957, his daughter Barbara, aged ten, who had been left alone all day, died of pneumonia. By then Ike was working in a warehouse at New Jersey's McGuire Air Force Base for $37 a week and living in an $11-a-week room at the YMCA.

Since 1965 Ike has been the boxing instructor to high school dropouts at the state-supported Camp Kilmer in Edison, New Jersey. The veteran of 155 professional fights is still a great fan and sees all the matches he can. "Boxing," he says, "has been very good to me." He has a room at the camp where he proudly displays the only relic left from his days of glory—the Lightweight Championship belt. He hopes eventually he can open a bar or liquor store in Trenton.

With Michael Knowles recently.
Diana Keyt

When she had the No. 1 record of 1940.

WEE BONNIE BAKER

The baby-voiced singing sensation was born Evelyn Nelson on April 1, 1917, in Orange, Texas. The nuns at the Ursuline Academy in Galveston and at the St. Agnes Academy in Houston taught her to play the ukelele and piano, but she picked up singing on her own. A local bandleader, Monk McCallister, heard her in a school play and obtained her parents' permission to feature the teen-ager with his group. They played the country club on weekends. By 1938, through a Houston booking agent, she was working at the Claridge Hotel, in St. Louis. Orrin Tucker, who was playing the same spot, offered her a job as vocalist with his band. He changed her name to Bonnie Baker and after a few months of teasing by the musicians about her height—four feet five inches—the "Wee" was added.

The Tucker aggregation toured for eighteen months before coming into Chicago's Palmer House. It was the time of the world premiere of the Alice Faye starrer *In Old Chicago* (1938) and department store windows and restaurants were going all out, reflecting the period of the movie—the time of the Great Fire. Tucker joined in and had Bonnie wear a bustle and picked for her a hit of 1917, "Oh, Johnny, Oh, Johnny, Oh," which she sang during the engagement and recorded in August, 1939. When they returned to Chicago after months of one-nighters, Bonnie found that her recording had swept the East Coast and was well on its way to becoming the top hit of 1940. Tucker and Bonnie were promptly signed by radio's "Your Hit Parade" and she sang her hit on a coast-to-coast hookup from where they were playing in San Antonio, Texas. *Time* magazine called her styling "melting and cajoling." One critic dubbed her sound "sex in a high chair."

186

Bonnie left Tucker in 1942, after her other hits, "Billy," "My Resistance Is Low," and "You'd Be Surprised," had made her such a hot property that no band leader could have afforded her. Bonnie was heard in presentation houses all over America, backed by such groups as Stan Kenton and Tony Pastor. She toured for the USO with an all-girl band and added another movie, *Spotlight Scandals* (1943) (an earlier one was *You're the One* [1941]). After the war Bonnie Baker was one of the stars of "Ken Murray's Blackouts" for a year, which is when she became close friends with the late Marie Wilson.[3] Marie was godmother to her only child, Sharon.

Bonnie worked during the 1950s at various clubs and cut an album for Warner Brothers in 1958. But as the musical tastes of the country changed, she found that she was singing louder and louder to compete with the cash register and the noise from the bar and the kitchen. Her bookings were not first class and some weren't even second class.

In 1950 she had married her accompanist, Billy Rogers, who also wrote some of comedian George Gobel's early material. Bonnie had a severe heart attack in 1963 and called a complete halt to a career that had already slowed to a standstill.

Wee Bonnie lives in Fort Lauderdale, Florida, with her husband and daughter. She admits missing the show people she enjoyed so much during her years at the top and could use the money. But she is afraid to chance a heavy schedule because of her heart, although she still smokes quite a bit. Last year she was offered an engagement with her old boss Orrin Tucker, but turned it down. Maybe she remembered the record he picked for her that skyrocketed her to fame. It sold 1½ million copies within the first year of its release but all she got was a flat fee of $10 and a set of matched luggage.

With her daughter Sharon in Fort Lauderdale, Florida. *Frank Redfield*

A "Beaver" publicity still, 1959.

JERRY MATHERS

The star of the television series "Leave It to Beaver" was born on June 2, 1948, in Sioux City, Iowa. By the time Jerry was two years old his family had moved to Los Angeles. One day when his mother had taken him shopping she was approached by the advertising director of the department store who asked if Jerry could model for their Christmas calendar. The photographer who took the photos suggested to Mrs. Mathers that she take Jerry to see a particular agent who specialized in children.

At the age of two and a half Jerry debuted on the late Ed Wynn's television show and then with his sister Susie played Faith Domergue's (married and living in Los Angeles) children in *This Is My Love* (1954). Alfred Hitchcock saw him on a Lux Video Theatre show and signed him for *The Trouble with Harry* (1955).

By the time Jerry was auditioned for the title role of Beaver Cleaver he had been seen with Bob Hope in *The Seven Little Foys* (1955) and *That Certain Feeling* (1956). The producers and director were impressed when Jerry told them that he hoped he could finish with the audition right away because he didn't want to be late for Cub Scout practice. That was exactly the sort of boy they conceived the character to be.

The program debuted on CBS Television on October 4, 1957, switching to NBC and finally ABC before it expired six years later into syndication, where it has remained ever since.

The situation comedy featured a respectful, well-meaning boy who usually through no fault of his own got into trouble. His "real" name on the series was Theodore, but almost everyone called him Beaver. There was an older brother, Wally, played by Tony Dow (who acts occasionally and sculpts with an acetylene torch) and their neighbor Eddie who took great pains to be very courteous to Beaver's parents but who was really the local troublemaker. That part was taken by Ken Osmond (now a Los Angeles police officer).

The show was produced by George Gobel's production company and although the cast worked five days a week turning out thirty-nine episodes a year, Jerry has admitted that his relationships with his TV family were always very businesslike and he seldom hears from them today. Barbara Billingsley played his mother, a character who seemed to respond emotionally to everything. Hugh Beaumont was Mr. Cleaver, a man with very fixed ideas about how boys should think and behave. Jerry's own father is a high school principal, and he used to take him crow shooting on weekends.

Jerry says he wasn't at all depressed when the show went off the networks, as by that time he had become very involved in his school sports program. Although he did a few guest appearances on such shows as "Batman" and "Lassie," he turned down many for fear they would interfere with his football and swimming practice.

At the height of the Vietnam War, a wire service story reported Jerry Mathers killed in action, and Shelley Winters repeated the news on a network talk show. Although the Mathers had a retraction out within twenty-four hours, many fans still believe Jerry is dead.

After graduating from high school in 1966 Jerry went into the Air Force, and is still a member of the Air National Guard, spending part of his summers on active duty. When not away at college he lives with his parents in Tarzana, California. Mathers's Beaver salary, which began at $500 a week, has been well invested. He doesn't feel troubled in any way for having been a TV star so young, and figures that because Beaver has such an All-American image he has not been typecast. He admits however that he will be fairly disappointed if, when he finishes his courses at University of California at Berkeley in philosophy and communications, he is unable to find work in television or "pitchers."

Today Jerry is a student and Air National Guardsman. *Brian Gari*

Miss Frances began and ended each "Ding Dong School" program by ringing her bell. *NBC*

MISS FRANCES OF "DING DONG SCHOOL"

Television's schoolmarm of the 1950s was born Frances Rappaport on July 16, 1908, in Ottawa, Ohio. The youngest of six children, she describes herself as a child dominated by seven bosses. Her father was inconsistent both with praise and discipline, and she learned early to play life's games. She would ask her mother for things her father had denied her. At school in the small town where she grew up, she was constantly compared with her brothers and sisters. "I found myself competing at home and in school for affection and attention," she said. "It made me at times hate everyone." One thing she resented most was having to wear hand-me-downs.

In 1929, she received a degree from the University of Chicago, and two years later married a teacher, Harvey L. Horwich. Frances also taught school, in Evanston, Illinois, until 1932. After that she was for three years a supervisor of schools in Chicago. She also holds degrees from Columbia and Northwestern. During her teaching years, Frances learned to lip-read.

Before stepping in front of the camera on October 3, 1952, for the premiere of "Ding Dong School," she heard a lighting technician say "If this show doesn't lay an egg, nothing ever will." The program lasted on the NBC network until 1956 and then went into syndication for another seven years. Its 2,800 half hours won thirty-five major awards, including four nominations for Emmys. In addition, there were seven Ding Dong School books and a series of LPs.

The show was the first slow-paced children's program, and it was geared to the preschool child. At its peak popularity, during the mid-1950s, Miss Frances received as many as 17,000 letters a day.

NBC's official reason for cancellation was a drop in the ratings, which for a time topped both Garry Moore's and Arthur Godfrey's, its rivals on CBS. The A. C. Nielsen ratings, which indicated that her listeners were starting grade school, and leaving their sets, did not consider the new families whose children were just coming of age for the series. However, Miss Frances believes that the network found women's programming to be much more profitable. And as the show's producer, she objected to commercials for products a child could not use.

After the show's demise, she returned to education but has occasionally produced specials for children (on WMAQ-TV in Chicago). And she has been a frequent guest on the "Sunday in Chicago" show.

Miss Frances does not believe in indoctrination. For example, in presenting a drawing, she was careful to draw two or three of everything so that the children would have choices. She also does not believe in sex education in schools before junior high.

Recently, when the Horwiches, who are childless, were dining near home in Chicago, a group of Ding Dongers now in their twenties surrounded their table and burst into the show's song: "I'm your school bell,/Ding, dong, ding./Boys and girls all hear me ring."

She was at first surprised and then felt very happy. "We had a wonderful visit with these young people. It makes me very proud to think that I had something to do with the forming of this splendid new generation."

During a rare TV appearance. *NBC*

With Lassie, 1955. *Jack Wrather Productions*

TOMMY RETTIG

Lassie's master was born Thomas Noel Rettig on December 10, 1941, in Jackson Heights, New York. A drama teacher who lived in his building wanted Tommy in her classes, but his parents were reluctant to spend money on what they thought was a very chancy profession. When he was five and a half years old, the teacher asked permission to take him to an audition for the part of Little Jake in the road company of *Annie Get Your Gun*. He was paid $60 a week for the forty-two-city tour starring Mary Martin. At the end of two years, the boy had still never seen a show from the audience.

From his role in that Irving Berlin musical, Tommy got work in such feature films as *Panic in the Streets* (1950), *Two Weeks with Love* (1950), *The Strip* (1951), and *Gobs and Gals* (1952). Then in 1953 he began playing Jeff on the first of television's "Lassie" series. When he was signed, he had never seen any of the Lassie movies. Nor had he read the books about the famous collie. But he spent the next five years on "Lassie," working about thirty weeks a year at $2,500 a week. He was replaced by Jon Provost (a college student in Northern California).

"Lassie" was both good and bad for Tommy, professionally and personally. Viewed by millions of Americans every Sunday evening, the show made Rettig one of Hollywood's hottest boy actors. He commanded top money for his roles in such movies as *So Big* (1953), *The 5,000 Fingers of Dr. T* (1953), and *The Egyptian* (1954) with Edmund Purdom (living in Rome). But he also soon realized that he was hopelessly typecast as an actor. After he was no longer a big TV star, parts were few and far between. Being five feet four inches didn't help either. His personal life was hurt by the

"Lassie" six-day-a-week shooting schedule. It restricted dating. "When I found that it was my last season I was ecstatic. I had gotten to the point where I really resented not being able to go out except on Saturday nights. Of course when I did date girls their parents always trusted me more because of my goody-goody TV image. The fools!" But he did develop close personal ties with Jan Clayton (his "mother") and the late George Cleveland (his "grandfather").

He made *River of No Return* (1954) with Marilyn Monroe and she got him an autographed baseball from Joe DiMaggio. His last movie was *The Last Wagon* (1956). His two big regrets are that his agents and parents turned down offers for him to play the lead in the Broadway company of *The Member of the Wedding* and the starring role in the film *Blue Denim*. Both went to the late Brandon de Wilde.

In 1959 Tommy married fifteen-year-old Darlene Portwood, whom he met while she was waiting for a bus. Tommy was her big crush in grammar school.

By 1966 Tommy had to face the fact that he simply could not make a living as an actor. His agent couldn't even get him bit parts, and Tommy tried selling menswear, working in an electronics shop, and a real estate office, but all of it bored him.

The city boy who became famous as a country kid now owns and operates the Daisy Hill Farm in Arroyo Grande, California. Along with his wife and two sons he farms organically on fifty acres, complete with rolling hills and a walnut grove. One of his crops was marijuana; a few days before Christmas, 1972, Tommy and Darlene were arrested by police acting on a tip from neighbors. But calls, letters, and wires from friends and fans all over the country poured in, offering help and good wishes. Many of them, including TV star Richard Deacon, offered to post bail.

As for sons Tommy and Dean wanting to act, (Dad won't even let them audition until they're out of high school), says Tommy: "I don't want them in studio schools. I can still barely read and write."

The Rettigs down on the farm today. *Sonny Landham*

In 1952, she was President Eisenhower's representative at the coronation of Elizabeth II. *UPI*

Still wearing the famous tinted glasses with the black frames. *Ene Riisna*

FLEUR COWLES

The once suprainfluential, envied, and imitated woman on Madison Avenue was born Fleur Fenton on January 20, 1910, in Montclair, New Jersey. When at the age of eleven she began to write she decided she would be a "great writer" like her idol Katherine Mansfield. After attending New York's School of Fine Arts she took a job as a copywriter for Gimbels department store. Before long she had her own ad agency, in Boston, but by 1932 was back in New York where she wrote a column, not unlike Lucius Beebe's, for the *World Telegram* for two years.

Also in 1932 she married Atherton Pettingell, and three years later they formed Dorland International, which, within a short period, became an important and lucrative advertising agency. Fleur really came into her own in the 1940s when during the war she served as a dollar-a-year executive giving lessons in speech writing to government and military bigwigs. She was the first female civilian to enter the liberated countries and was on a first-name basis with many of the country's most powerful men. In December of 1946, following her divorce earlier in the year, she married Gardner

Cowles, the publishing magnate, and set about to change *Look* from a barbershop sheet into a respectable family magazine. Within two years *Look*'s circulation soared, and ad lineage doubled. She is also credited as having inspired *Quick*, in 1949, a pocket-size pictorial that for a brief existence did rather well. But in the process she made more enemies than she would ever know. Fleur Cowles became the media monster of the moment, the person one was supposed to hate. However, George Eells, who had been on her staff and later wrote biographies of Cole Porter, Hedda Hopper, and Louella Parsons, remembers her as exacting and demanding but frank and scrupulously fair.

Fleur's real triumph, of which she is justly proud, is *Flair,* a publishing legend. Cowles gave her a large budget and a free hand to produce the most beautiful, eclectic monthly ever seen in the United States. For thirteen issues beginning in January, 1950, she presented the arts, literature, humor, fashion, travel, and entertainment—all on pages of different sizes, colors, and textures. It featured the first double foldout cover, die cuts, and a new binding method. Although the magazine ceased publication after its January, 1951, issue, it is still copied by the slick monthlies, and the old issues bring top prices among periodicals collectors.

During her heyday, Fleur seemed to be everywhere and with everybody. She even flew her own plane. Her trademarks were the ash blonde hair and horn-rimmed glasses tinted to shield her light-sensitive eyes. One of her closest friends was Bernard Baruch, of whom she says: "He expected me to know everything." He would call her almost daily and question her. "I spent years of my life trying not to let him down," Fleur has said. One of the books she wrote is *Bloody Predecent* (1952), a comparative study of two Argentinian dictatorships, which included an excellent character study of Eva Perón.

In 1955, Fleur gave Cowles the divorce he asked for, moved to London, and married English millionaire Tom Montague Meyer. A book of her experiences with some of the famous personalities she has known—written at the encouragement of her late friend Isak Dinesen—will be published in England. But the great goal of her life lies elsewhere and she is concentrating her considerable energies on painting. Her oils line the walls of her several residences—in her flat in the historic Albany apartments smack in the middle of Piccadilly, in her country home in Sussex, and in the twelfth century castle she and her husband recently purchased in a remote area of Spain.

Of Women's Lib, although she is all for equal pay, "I think we get much farther by being needed and seeming feminine," she concludes. She visits the United States but avoids New York: "I'm afraid I'm rather scared by my experience with fame in New York. I'm much more sensitive than a lot of people think and it hurt me very much when I was called, by people I've never met, 'the hatchet woman at *Look*.' It just so happens that Mike Cowles ran *Look*. I want a private life. Here one is allowed that luxury. They're not impressed with minor accomplishments. I remain a U.S. citizen but my home is here."

He was on the first Kraft Music
Hall televised, 1948. *NBC*

DOODLES WEAVER

The hayseed comic from early television was born Winstead Sheffield
Glendening Dixon Weaver in Los Angeles in 1914. His father was the
wealthy industrialist who founded the All-Year Club that promoted the
area's climate and attracted millions to the state in the thirties and forties.
His brother is "Pat" Sylvester Weaver, the media executive and former
president of NBC.

Because of his freckles and big ears, Winstead's mother began calling him
her "doodle bug." Doodles's original goal was to become a school athletic
director, but the money he made working in Andy Clyde and Three Stooges
shorts hooked him on movies and comedy. He played a farmer in *Topper*
(1937), his first feature, and after a few more small parts as a hick he got
the reputation as the poor man's Sterling Holloway.[3] He was Hannibal
Hoops in the early version of *Li'l Abner* (1940) and played a wounded
sailor in *The Story of Dr. Wassell* (1944).

Doodles's first real prominence was as Professor Feedelbaum with the
Spike Jones band for three years, beginning in 1948. He was with Spike's
City Slickers on their radio show, records, and national tours of presentation
houses. He left them when someone at NBC got the idea of starring him in
a summer replacement series after seeing his Ajax commercial (on a "Colgate Comedy Hour" show), in which he used a live pig.

On the NBC program, which was televised the summer of 1951, Doodles
wore crazy costumes, did his bumpkin character, and emitted just about
every strange and vulgar sound ever heard. A lot of people found him

funny. One who didn't was columnist Jack O'Brian, who over and over rapped the show's mindlessness, including the humor, which he felt was forced.

A local "Day with Doodles" followed the NBC program on New York City's Channel 5 for a short time, and then Weaver returned to Hollywood. For a couple of years in the late fifties on Channel 2 in Los Angeles his Doodles Club House was popular on Saturday mornings, and then he hosted a kiddie program on a San Francisco station for a season.

Since his heyday as a TV personality Doodles has been a busy actor. But in his small and frequently serious roles on TV and in feature films, he is seldom recognized by the audiences. He was a murderer in *Winchester "73"* (1950), and he was the boatowner in a tense scene in Hitchcock's *The Birds* (1963). In the late fifties he had a running part as the hotel owner in the "Lawman" series on television.

Just mentioning his name on TV can still get a big laugh but no one will book him as a guest. When in June, 1972, he broke the world's record throwing a javelin in the Senior Citizen Olympics, he called all the talk shows about appearing. One producer said he never heard of him. Another said, "Oh yeah. You're Pat Weaver's brother, right?" Someone from the "Tonight Show" said to him, "We really love you but can't figure out what to do with you."

Doodles's marriages have ended in three divorces and one annulment. His last wife was twenty-one years old. He now lives alone in his North Hollywood quarters, where among his three cars is a pre-World War II LaSalle.

He doesn't seem to miss being a star. "I don't miss anything because I live in the now. I haven't had a drink in five years and I don't even miss that. I don't have any money. Even my Cadillac is a 1956 model but the highlights of my life were not in front of a camera. My happiest times came when I made a tackle in the All-Star football game playing for Stanford and when I was named Best Student Athlete at my school, Irving Preparatory in Tarrytown, New York."

Still mugging. *Richard Schaeffer*

A distressed Blanche in *Cry of the Werewolf* (1944).

BLANCHE YURKA

The stage star–movie character actress was born in June, 1887, in St. Paul, Minnesota, to Bohemian immigrants. Her earliest ambition was to sing opera, so her father squeezed the family budget while Blanche took singing lessons at 75 cents a week.

The Yurkas moved to New York, where in 1904 Blanche debuted as a flower girl in the Metropolitan Opera school's production of *Parsifal.* "After that," says Blanche, "all the success I hoped for, and knew would come to me, happened." By 1907 her operatic career was forgotten and she was playing on Broadway in *The Warrens of Virginia.* She made friends with the star, Jane Cowl, who encouraged her and helped her choose clothes, arrange interviews, and meet the right people.

Blanche's first great success was as Queen Gertrude in the 1922 Broadway production of *Hamlet,* which starred John Barrymore in the title role. She eventually developed a reputation for interpretation of the classics, and scored great successes with her Broadway appearances in *The Wild Duck* (1925), *Goat Song* (1926), and *Hedda Gabler* (1929). During these years she was married briefly to actor Ian Keith, several years her junior: "It wasn't the age thing that broke us up. It was professional insecurity."

Because of her lectures on the theatre around the country and her many national tours with plays, Blanche became one of the best known stage stars of her day. Unlike many stars, Blanche *liked* the road. Her career has always come before her private life and she has no regrets about that order.

Although she has appeared in over twenty motion pictures, she will discuss only *A Tale of Two Cities* (1935), in which she played Madame Defarge. Some of her pictures are *Queen of the Mob* (1940), *The Song of Bernadette* (1943), *The Bridge of San Luis Rey* (1944), *The Flame* (1947), and *The Furies* (1950).

Two of the three great disappointments of her life were movie parts she didn't get. She wanted very much to play Luise Rainer's[1] part in *The Good Earth* (1937). When (Alla) Nazimova was offered *For Whom the Bell Tolls* (1943), she suggested Blanche do it, but Paramount gave it to Katrina Paxinou, who won an Oscar for her efforts. "And she was superb," said Blanche many years later. "But then I might have been superb, too." Blanche's last disappointment came in 1969 when she played the title role in an off-Broadway production of *The Madwoman of Chaillot*. It was dismissed by the critics. The *New York Times* published her letter shortly afterward in which she bid farewell to New York audiences.

A large woman, she has a compelling personality off-stage as well as on. Particularly to an older generation, Blanche Yurka sounds (her voice developed over the many years that microphones were unknown in theatres), looks, and conducts herself like a great actress.

For a star who epitomizes an era long gone in the theatre, Blanche is startlingly modern in her ideas. She welcomes the deemphasizing of glamour in characterizations and publicity: "I never met a single person who really lived the way the public believed we lived." And she is happy with the revolution in plays and acting styles: "The parts are real today and the actors are natural. We were so affected!"

Miss Yurka, who says that if she were young today she would never marry but would live with the man instead, preferably a younger man, walks with the aid of two canes. She lives alone on Manhattan's East 72nd Street in a cooperative apartment she bought many years ago; its furnishings could have come from the set of one of her early plays. One of her close friends over the years is the film and stage actor Romney Brent (retired and living in Mexico City). She still appears from time to time at womens' clubs and colleges in a program of readings, and in 1970 published her autobiography, *Bohemian Girl.*

In her large Manhattan co-op apartment. *Peaches Poland*

In 1934, a matinee idol on stage and in movies.

FRANCIS LEDERER

The Czech leading man of stage and screen was born Frantisek Lederer on November 6, 1906, in Prague. As a young man, he worked his way through the Prague Academy of Dramatic Arts by dressing windows for a department store and then toured Eastern and Central Europe for several years with a repertory company. He was first leading man with the Burg Theatre in Vienna, when Max Reinhardt brought him to Berlin in 1930 to play Romeo to Elisabeth Bergner's[1] Juliet. By then he had been seen with Louise Brooks[3] in the silent classic, *Pandora's Box* (1929), and in *The Wonderful Lie of Nova Petrowa* (1930), and was the rage of German and French cinema audiences.

Lederer's big success, one he was never able to equal, was *Autumn Crocus,* which he first did in London in 1931, to rave notices. He and the play were imported to Broadway, opening November 19, 1932. The production was one of the highlights of the season and his subsequent tour with it was a triumph. Francis was signed for motion pictures and everyone expected the handsome young man with the charming accent to become a major star in the United States. It never happened.

In Hollywood, he made *Pursuit of Happiness* (1934), *My American Wife* (1936), and *The Lone Wolf in Paris* (1938). He was fine in all of them; also in *The Man I Married* (1940), with Anna Sten,[1] and *The Diary of a Chambermaid* (1946), with Hurd Hatfield (living in Stony Brook, New York). But the only time he really registered on screen was in *Confessions of a Nazi Spy* (1939).

Lederer was a dedicated actor but there was talk of temperament, as when his scheduled appearance in *Break of Hearts* was cancelled by RKO. What was more likely is that in pictures he simply lacked the sex appeal that was so evident on stage. Certainly he couldn't have been very temperamental or choosy about what he did after *The Bridge of San Luis Rey* (1944) —a Republic cheapie, *The Madonna's Secret* (1946), with Linda Stirling (living in North Hollywood, where she is a schoolteacher), *Million Dollar Weekend* (1949), with Gene Raymond (living in Westwood Village, California), *Captain Carey, U.S.A.* (1950), with Wanda Hendrix (married and living in Sherman Oaks), and *The Ambassador's Daughter* (1956).

During his picture-making days, Lederer returned to the stage occasionally, in 1939 taking over for Laurence Olivier in *No Time For Comedy*, on Broadway, and in various road companies such as *Watch on the Rhine* and *The Diary of Anne Frank*. And he was still a big draw on European stages following the end of World War II. Two of his last screen appearances were in title roles in *The Return of Dracula* (1958), with Ray Stricklyn (living in Los Angeles), and the critical and financial dud, *The Legend of Lylah Claire* (1968).

Lederer lives with his third wife, socialite Marion Irvine, in a large home that resembles an old mission—embellished with antique Spanish furniture. Marion was preceded by opera singer Ada Miedly and Margo (married to Eddie Albert). Lederer is honorary mayor of Canoga Park, California, perhaps because he owns so much of it. The Lederers gave much of their property to the county for a public park, which still leaves them with 250 acres for themselves.

Not only isn't Francis bitter over what didn't happen with his career; he seems disinterested in it. Perhaps it is because he was so well paid for his efforts. The money, shrewdly invested, provides him with time for his pet interest—the Workshop 70 theatre and dance school in North Hollywood, where he often lectures and teaches what he did so well—acting.

In the North Hollywood acting school where he sometimes teaches.
Shifra Haran

In 1933, Blossom made her one feature film, *Broadway Thru a Keyhole*.

BLOSSOM SEELEY

The superstar of vaudeville was born in San Pueblo, California, in 1891. She began singing professionally between acts at the San Francisco Repertory Theatre, then under the direction of Sid Grauman. Lew Fields heard her and brought Blossom to Broadway to be with Weber and Fields in *The Hen-Pecks* in 1911.

The next year she was in *Charity Girl* and then *Whirl of Society* with Al Jolson. In 1915 she was featured along with Marion Davies in Irving Berlin's *Stop! Look! Listen!*

Blossom hit her stride in vaudeville. She was small, cute, and had a voice that could be heard in the third balcony. Some of the songs she introduced and/or popularized are "The Japanese Sandman," "Smiles," "Way Down Yonder in New Orleans," and "California, Here I Come." She got top billing at New York's Palace and everywhere else she played. She had particularly good relations with the press and was known on stage and off for her chic clothes.

Her personal life was quite another matter. In 1913 her first husband, Joseph Kane, sued baseball star Rube Marquand for alienation of Blossom's affections. Blossom divorced Kane and married the athlete, but that union also ended in divorce, on grounds of desertion. In 1920 while playing Chicago, Blossom met Benny Fields, a singer several years her junior who had had no success up until then. They were married in 1921 and one way or another were together until he died in 1959.

The pair worked constantly through the twenties headlining vaudeville bills and such shows as the Greenwich Village Follies of 1928. Although he improved a great deal over the years, there was always something embarrassing about a man of Fields's ability sharing the spotlight with a star of Blossom's stature. He was well aware that many called him "Mr. Blossom Seeley" but he loved performing even more than Blossom, and if a booker wanted her he would have to take Fields as well.

In 1934 Fields went out as a single and Blossom announced that he was going to be the star of the family from then on. He enjoyed a brief success but soon was reduced to accepting the billing of "formerly with Blossom Seeley."

They had been out of the limelight for quite a few years when Paramount filmed a musical version of their lives, starring Betty Hutton and Ralph Meeker. *Somebody Loves Me* (1952) was such a success there was talk of a sequel, and Seeley and Fields were booked into clubs like the Cocoanut Grove, where they did more business than Frank Sinatra. They had a disc jockey show on WMGM in New York, made numerous TV appearances, and cut a new album, *Two a Day at the Palace.*

In 1952 she was feted by the Friars Club, thereby becoming the first woman ever to set foot inside it. She was also the first woman to sing the blues in Carnegie Hall, in 1925.

Blossom never considered herself retired and was working on her memoirs when, in 1968, she broke her hip in a fall. After months in a hospital, she was moved to a nursing home in Manhattan, which she has never left.

The star who was not only a great favorite with the public but personally among show people is very much alone. Ed Sullivan, who featured her and Fields often on his TV show, and George Burns, a lifelong friend, have visited her only once. The one contemporary she hears from regularly is Ruth Etting, who writes to her from the West Coast.

Now in a nursing home. *Antoinette Lopopolo*

Pete *(right)* signing up Dave O'Brien to a long-term contract, 1945.
D. Victorek

PETE SMITH

The creator of the Pete Smith Specialties was born on September 4, 1892, in the Hell's Kitchen section of New York City. Willing but unable (because he was frail) to hold his own in street fights, Pete began reading everything he could get his hands on.

He attended business college and worked as a stenographer and file clerk in an import house for three years at a starting salary of $6 a week. He read every theatrical trade paper of the day, and in 1910 landed an office job with the White Rats, a theatrical union. Soon he was transferred to their house organ, *The Player,* where he was a reporter and ad salesman. Smith played the drums in a band he had during this period. After working for a time as movie editor and critic on *Billboard,* he became assistant to Harry Reichenbach, an ace press agent of the day.

He remained a press agent for more than two decades and was with Famous-Players Lasky (which became Paramount Pictures), represented director Marshall Neilan, and Douglas Fairbanks, Sr., eventually opening his own offices.

He went with M-G-M as head of publicity before being put in charge of advertising. Then, in 1931, Louis B. Mayer tapped him to write and narrate Metro's factual short subjects. At first Pete worked on their *Sports Champions* and *Fisherman's Paradise* series, which is where he developed some of his techniques, such as running film inverted and backward and using absurd sound effects. He also did a series of ten *Goofy Movies* in which he

204

utilized stock footage, silent comedies, and old newsreels. In 1935 he was rewarded with his own series, *Pete Smith Specialties.*

The films were brought in for about $20,000 each, high for a short subject, but so profitable for the studio that the series continued until 1955, long after most shorts production had been halted. One, *Audioscopiks* (1935), which was an *M-G-M Special* Smith made for $11,000, grossed over $300,000 just in North America. Smith's economy and imagination enabled him to keep high production values throughout, including some use of costly Technicolor.

It was the Pete Smith personality that made the shorts unique. In his narration he mused on life's minor frustrations and aggravations, but he and the audience always laughed with the victim, not at him. Smith, who never appeared in any of his films, sounded like someone everyone knew. Neither his humor nor his voice was ever criticized as slick.

Smith's "victim" was almost always the late Dave O'Brien, who Pete has called "the No. 1 fall guy of the movies" because of all the stunts O'Brien did in the shorts. O'Brien's leading lady many times was his wife, Dorothy Short, and O'Brien himself doubled as a writer and idea man. He spent the last years of his life as a gag man for Red Skelton.

Two of those who directed some of the shorts before going on to bigger things are George Sidney and Fred Zinnemann. Don DeFore and Margaret Hamilton (living in Manhattan's Gramercy Park district) are among the actors seen in some of the 209 films.

Pete's years as a movie maker of shorts earned him twenty Oscar nominations, two of which he won. A third was presented to him when he retired, "for his witty and pungent observations of the American scene." The only reason he quit was because of a heart condition, and he has taken it easy ever since. He plays golf, "be it ever so lousy," tends to his rose garden, and works on a book about his years as a press agent for silent stars. He still sees a lot of movies. He married his former secretary in 1962, four years after the death of his first wife.

In the backyard of his Beverly Hills home. *Malcolm Leo*

In 1952 he celebrated the twentieth anniversary of his program on NBC.

CARLTON E. MORSE

The creator-writer of "One Man's Family," the longest running serial in radio history, was born on June 4, 1901, in Jennings, Louisiana, and was brought up on a farm in southern Oregon. He left the University of California after two and a half years of poor grades and worked for a number of newspapers. Thereafter, in 1929, he joined NBC in San Francisco as a staff producer-writer.

The first man at the network to consider his idea for a show on the fictional Barbours, an upper-middle-class family living in the Sea Cliff area of San Francisco, could see no appeal in it, and he felt that Morse was "written out." But another executive approved its being tried over NBC's West Coast network. On April 29, 1932, at 9:30 P.M. P.S.T. began the program that was "dedicated to the mothers and fathers of the younger generation and their bewildering offspring." It lasted the Depression, World War II, and the Eisenhower era, ending with Chapter 30 of Book 134 on May 8, 1959. But by then, Morse, whose inspiration derived from Galsworthy's *The Forsyte Saga,* was well into its TV version, which had begun in 1949.

Morse knew most of his actors personally and wrote, and usually directed, their parts to complement their true personalities. His development of characters through marriage, death, birth, and tragedy has never been equaled in radio or TV writing, and within the trade earned for the Barbours the title "First Family of Radio." Morse still receives a great deal of mail inquiring about the fictional family, as though they were real people.

Mother and Father Barbour (Minetta Ellen and J. Anthony Smythe) are deceased. Paul (Michael Raffetto) lives in Berkeley. Hazel (Mrs. A. Brooks Berlin) is in Oakland. She was the mother of twins Pinky and Hank (Dix

Davis, a State Department official and Billy Idelson, producer of TV's "Anna and the King" series). The original Claudia is married and living in the Virgin Islands. Page Gilman, Jack (brother of Claudia) from the first to the last broadcast, lives in Watsonville, California.

On January 16, 1939, Morse introduced a totally different series, "I Love a Mystery," which was heard at different times on three networks. Also expertly written, the blood curdler was so successful the Nicaraguan government once lodged a protest against one of the stories; also, an inmate at the Colorado state prison's death row spent his last minutes before going to the gas chamber listening to one of its episodes. Mercedes McCambridge was one of the regular cast members of "I Love a Mystery."

Though casual listeners to "One Man's Family" might have complained about nothing much happening, for the millions who planned their evenings around the program, Morse had caught the pace and basic character of Middle America. The comedy team Bob and Ray parodied the Barbours with their skit, "One Fella's Family," in which nothing ever happened, but Morse even now commands awesome respect in the media for having made more Americans happy, sad, and scared than any other writer at a time when people were desperate for diversion.

Morse feels we haven't changed so much since the Barbours reigned on NBC as we have become less naive. Far from intolerant of today's youth, he feels that young people leave home and try new ways because when they look to their families for love, they find none.

Morse has all the 3,256 scripts he wrote for "One Man's Family," including recordings of many of the programs. The recordings are being taped and will be distributed by the Perkins School for the Blind. He writes daily—novels, which he doesn't care if they never get published.

On holidays the fictional Barbours would visit their country house, down the coast from San Francisco. It was rustic and surrounded by trees and they called it Sky Ranch. Morse and his wife actually built such a house many years ago and that is where they live, in Woodside, California. He belongs to the Explorers Club.

During a recent trip to San Francisco. *Jimmy Eason*